Stray Leaves

Also by John Hanson Mitchell

Ceremonial Time

Living at the End of Time

A Field Guide to Your Own Backyard

Walking Towards Walden

Trespassing

Following the Sun

The Wildest Place on Earth

Looking for Mr. Gilbert

The Rose Café

The Paradise of All These Parts: A Natural History of Boston

The Last of the Bird People

An Eden of Sorts: A Natural History of My Feral Garden

Stray Leaves

Selected Essays from *Sanctuary* Magazine

by John Hanson Mitchell

Illustrated

Published by the
Massachusetts Audubon Society
Lincoln, MA 01773

Published by the
Massachusetts Audubon Society as a benefit of membership, 2015

Copyright 2015 by the Massachusetts Audubon Society
ISBN 978-0-9863869-1-6

Designer: Lynne Foy
Copyeditor: Ann Prince
Production Manager: Rose Murphy
Cover Artists: Leslie Watkins (front) Autumn; James Coe (back) Spring Evening
Proofreaders: Janet Foster, Betty Graham

Mass Audubon works to protect the nature of Massachusetts for people and wildlife. Together with more than 100,000 members, we care for 35,000 acres of conservation land; provide school, camp, and other educational programs for 225,000 children and adults annually; and advocate for sound environmental policies at local, state, and federal levels. Founded in 1896 by two inspirational women who were committed to the protection of birds, Mass Audubon is now one of the largest and most prominent conservation organizations in New England. Today we are respected for our sound science, successful advocacy, and innovative approaches to connecting people and nature. Each year, our statewide network of wildlife sanctuaries welcomes nearly half a million visitors of all ages, abilities, and backgrounds and serves as the base for our work. To support these important efforts, call 800-AUDUBON (800-283-8266) or visit www.massaudubon.org.

Acknowledgements and Notes About Sanctuary Magazine

Although they appear over my name, this collection of essays, garnered from the first edition of *Sanctuary* in August of 1980 to the final edition in July of 2014, was not the work of a sole individual. All I did was write them. But their publication, from concept to final print, was the assembled work of others, so many in fact that I would never be able to recall who did what, with which issue, or where such and such an idea came from. But there are a few individuals, both current and past, who over the years have contributed in a variety of ways, with background information, ideas, and the actual production.

The main body of the production work, and the most consistent, has been the work of the recent *Sanctuary* staff, associate editor Ann Prince and production editor Rose Murphy. Ann worked on *Sanctuary* at various levels for over 27 years, and Rose has been seeing to many details of production for 12 years. But there were others before that. Betty Graham, the former managing editor and a current proofreader for this book, worked on the publication for 13 years. And before Ann, Gretchen Flock was the copyeditor. She was there at the very beginning and is still a sharp-eyed reader. It says something about either the journal or the working conditions that over the 34 years of publication and 200 editions that there have been very few staff members—not a lot of turnover, in other words. Other long-term staff people include the freelance designers. There have been only two in the entire 34-year run, Lynne Foy, and before her, Valerie Bessette.

The other people who helped with the various themes, and to some extent the essays, were the writers who contributed to *Sanctuary*, some of whom have been writing for the magazine since the earliest editions. A few of these regulars were staff people. Chris Leahy wrote columns for the journal off and on up to the end. Simon Perkins used to write a very popular bird column. And other staff members in various fields have contributed stories (as well as essay ideas). These include, in no particular order, Charles Roth, Wayne Petersen, Robert Buchsbaum, Joe Choiniere, René Laubach, and Ann Prince, who wrote both feature stories and columns over the years, and the various writers, including Heidi Ricci and the Public Policy staff who put together "The Political Landscape" column.

But quite apart from the staff members, and equally helpful with essay ideas, were the freelance writers. Tom Conuel, the field editor, was the longest associate; he began writing for Mass Audubon before there even was a *Sanctuary*, and was still writing for the magazine to the end. The other loyal contributor, Gayle Goddard Taylor, also a field editor, came up with her own good story ideas once she learned of the theme of a particular issue. Both Tom and Gayle are journalists by trade, and as a result they were able to write about almost any subject, given the time to do the research.

The other regular freelancers often had a special field. Anytime I had an idea for a story involving plants I would call Teri Chace, or, for insects (or almost any nature subject for that matter), Michael Caduto, or for gardens, Dori Smith, and Karl Meyer was the river contact. And finally, I had a huge "stable," as it is called in the trade, of other freelance generalists. These include (again in no particular order) over the course of the life of the journal: Nini Bloch, Deborah Cramer, David Foster, Robert Finch, David Gessner, Cliff Hauptman, Jerry Howard, Richard Walton, Gail McClelland Fenton, Paul Karr, Jack Thorndike, Lois Josimovich, Bill Kirk, Tom Palmer, Bill Scheller, Melissa Stewart, Ann Taylor, Dexter Van Zile, and Ted Williams. For years Genie Zeiger was the poetry editor for the magazine (the first in fact), followed by coeditors Susan Richmond and Wendy Drexler.

I also had a long-lived group of regular illustrators whose work accompanied various stories over the years. The most enduring was Gordon Morrison, who did freelance work for Mass Audubon before there was a *Sanctuary* magazine and was with us to the end. He began by illustrating the earlier publication, *The Curious Naturalist*, and then continued doing the annotated illustrations as a single page in *Sanctuary*. He also frequently illustrated articles. Another earlier contributor was Michael DiGiorgio who specialized in bird illustrations. Other regulars had specific subjects. Barry Van Dusen, although versatile with many subjects, was a regular bird art contributor. Robert Seaman specialized in fish illustrations, and

Richard Sardinha had a talent for cold-blooded beasts, everything from insects and amphibians to reptiles and fish. He could also render fine illustrations of prehistory animals such as the woolly mammoth. Rob Dunlavey specialized in editorial art and Mary Newell DePalma did many of the animal images. These were only the regulars. There were many others who did black-and-white spot illustrations for the publication before we added color. Some of these appear on the pages of this book. There were so many over so many years, we're unable to credit them all.

Although they might not have realized it at the time, all these people, via conversations over the story ideas, contributed to the essays that appear in this book in one way or another.

I may not have realized either, but without them there would not have been a *Sanctuary* magazine.

Artists for this edition:

Steve Anderson
David M. Carroll
Mary Newell DePalma
Michael DiGiorgio
Don Eckelberry
William S. Fowler
Charles H. Joslin
Armin Landeck
James A. Mitchell
Gary MacDonald
Gordon Morrison
Michael Musto
Carol O'Malia

Laurel Molk
Emily Osman
Ann Prince
Alexandra Schultz
Robert Seaman
Ernest H. Shepard
J. Fletcher Street
George Miksch Sutton
Abby A. Gove Tenney
T. Wellman
Brenton Welsh
Francis Willughby

Foreword

If Mass Audubon were to sell the movie rights to *Stray Leaves*, the opening scene could show us a wild-haired man lying in a grassy field, gazing upward at the evening sky, watching bats in the fading light. One flutter-winged flier grows larger and larger—an enormous bat? The man starts up in surprise, then relaxes. In a tone of quiet happiness he mutters, "Nighthawk."

As the credits roll we see a montage of images: a golden fox at large on a small island, then the surrounding water fading to land, the island to water. Then in darkness, we return to water, this time a sheltered bay where a small schooner is anchored. The sky is filled with a shower of meteors, and a sailor, the brother of the man with untamed locks, executes an arching dive from the crosstrees of the mast. His splash answers the falling stars with upward-shooting bioluminescence, which dissolves to fireflies seen from a porch, where a boy sits among gathered cousins, listening to his father spin a yarn about the intriguing flashing insects.

As the film proceeds there are more scenes. Our protagonist is obviously struck through with curiosity. He wants a deep experience in nature: to know its science and to absorb its spirit. Tramping outdoors with aged men and women, he shares their regret at the loss of a world more personal, authentic, and unhurried than the one they've come to inhabit.

Stray Leaves would not play in your local multiplex. You'd see it in a smaller, quieter venue, suitable for contemplation, where a congenial sage could rise up to inform us that our fascination with technology and commerce ought to be balanced with a love of the land and its animals and plants. Ought to for humanity's own well-being and for the sake of other forms of life that have as much right as we do to inherit the Earth, if not more, being our elders.

The essays collected here were first published in *Sanctuary*, which was the magazine of the Massachusetts Audubon Society from 1980 to 2014. Wayne Hanley was publications director, when, in 1972, he hired John Hanson Mitchell to write white papers on environmental subjects. When Wayne retired, John was asked to create a new publication for Mass Audubon, and *Sanctuary* was the result. It built on models from past publications by combining natural history with reporting on environmental issues and by having a theme for each issue. John introduced each edition with a short, sometimes oblique essay based on the theme. This collection is a selection of those essays, which are the thoughts of a man awake to nature, literature, and imagination.

I joined Mass Audubon at the beginning of the *Sanctuary* era, when I returned from two years away, teaching at an outdoor education center in Texas. Hungry as I was to learn New England's natural history, the works of Hanley and Mitchell were like a table set for me. When *Sanctuary* came in the mail, I read it cover to cover, and I devoured M.R. Montgomery's nature columns in the *The Boston Globe* and studied R.T. Peterson's *Field Guide to Eastern Birds*.

Sanctuary was beautifully designed and rich in prose, poems, and pictures. The JHM essays set the tone and wove the series of themes into a fabric. As time went by, we gained a sense of auditing a long, varied narrative by a writer who seemed to have traveled everywhere and to have read everything, but whose chief sources of meaning and joy were right in front of us, accessible to all willing to take time and pay attention.

Mass Audubon published *Sanctuary* for 34 years—all under John's editorship. Issues have been entered into the Congressional Record. They have played a part in any number of local environmental tussles. One of John's essays was turned into a school play. The deposition by the animal kingdom against the hegemony of our species was the basis for a church service. His *Sanctuary* pieces have appeared on the op-ed pages of the *The Boston Globe* and *The New York Times* and have been republished by smaller journals. His essay "Of Time and the River" won the John Burroughs Medal.

During the years he was editing *Sanctuary*, John was also writing books. His first, *Ceremonial Time*, has become a classic in the American literature of place and a model for accounts by other authors of a square mile's passage through time.

It was an "Editor's Choice" in *The New York Times Book Review*, has appeared as four editions, and spawned a series of five books now collected together and republished as the Scratch Flat Chronicles. John's eleven books examine the various cultural, environmental, and historical subjects through a close look at a specific patch of geography. While most can be classed in the literature of place, one is a biography of the first African American landscape photographer and many are memoirs—all of his writing is personal.

Through *Sanctuary* John extended a rich Massachusetts heritage. Ralph Waldo Emerson wrote *Nature* on the banks of the Sudbury River. In seeking wisdom and nourishment from the natural world, Emerson was followed by Massachusetts naturalists Henry David Thoreau, William Brewster, Ludlow Griscom, and Allen Morgan, a human chain described by Richard K. Walton in the first section of *Birds of the Sudbury River Valley*, which Mass Audubon published in 1984, the same year Doubleday released *Ceremonial Time*.

Sanctuary was nurtured and powered by a wealth of talent that emerged in the last decades of the past century—writers, illustrators, photographers, and the magazine's interminable staff—who celebrated nature. Contributing to *Sanctuary* placed them in the Massachusetts Thoreauvian tradition. Some cheered and abetted the surging popularity of birding, but less glamorous life-forms also received attention, as did the history of our landscape.

Although John is concerned with values and expresses worry about our priorities as a society, he avoids sanctimony, revels in irony, and knows that appearances can deceive. In the essay "Saving Graces," John braces himself because he thinks he's about to witness the squashing of a turtle by a youngish man at the wheel of a muscle car. Instead, that driver slams on the brakes, jumps out of his car, and tenderly carries the animal to safety, as he informs John: "Spotted turtle. These are rare. We've got to take care of these guys."

Stray Leaves, the movie, might end on such a hopeful note. Or it could show us pleading nolo contendere in the animals' court. But in the finale I'd prefer we see our author at the edge of his garden, in dappled sunlight, writing on a pad of paper. A winged beauty distracts him by landing at the tip of his pen. John's reaction: "Prose is but words—a dragonfly tops it all."

Ron McAdow
Massachusetts writer Ron McAdow is a former director of Sudbury Valley Trustees and a longtime member of Mass Audubon.

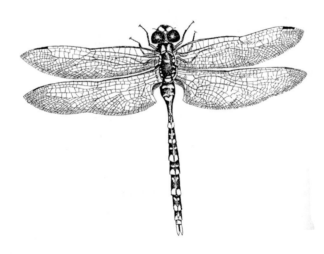

Blues in the Night

Could they have known the details, the ancient Greeks would have appreciated the life cycle of the blue-spotted salamander. For eleven and a half months of the year, the blue-spot is a dweller in the nether regions of the earth. It lurks in dank, sunless holes, two to four feet beneath the surface of the woodland floor, feeding on sow bugs, worms, and other subterranean creatures. Once a year, generally on the darkest, wettest nights of late March or early April, it emerges from the underworld to migrate through the rainy woods to temporary ponds, where it courts, mates, and lays its eggs. Then, its mission in the upper world complete, it crawls determinedly back through the forest to its hole for the remainder of the year.

The obscure night migration of the blue-spot has all the mythic elements the Greeks so loved, and even in our hedonistic and decidedly profane era, their dark existence holds a certain fascination. It is unfortunate that, like so many meaningful natural events in our time, this little drama may be threatened by current industrial processes.

There was a temporary pond not far from a house I once lived in, a shallow, rounded pool hidden below the ridge of a small hill at the end of a dirt road. Each spring, on the first rainy nights of April, the black waters of that pond would be alive with the thrashing bodies of male blue-spotted salamanders desperately attempting to attract the attention of the females. Students who visited the pond during the late 1960s counted more than 50 individuals on one night; it was clearly an important breeding pool and probably had been ever since the glacier withdrew from the Northeast some 12,000 years ago.

During the early 1970s, a biology professor from a nearby university noticed a decline in the population of the species in that particular pond, and during subsequent years the numbers dwindled even more, so that by 1976 only one lone male remained in the pond. In 1978 he too disappeared.

As it turned out, herpetologists throughout the Northeast had noticed similar drops in salamander populations in the region, and by 1977 it was determined from several separate studies that, in effect, events taking place in the Midwest were killing off the salamanders of New England. Acid precipitation caused by stack emissions in the industrial triangle created by the cities of Chicago, Detroit, and Pittsburg were creating a chemical imbalance in the waters of the ponds where the salamanders breed and thereby killing the embryos. Blue-spotted salamanders are now considered rare in many Northeastern states.

It may seem of little import to the world at large that unless some substantial changes are made in the political sphere in the next few years the blue-spotted may disappear from the woodlands of the Northeast, and possibly from the world. Salamanders, after all, appear to have very little to do with the general course of things: human affairs continue, wars and rumors  of wars flare and settle, and it may seem that the decline of the blue-spotted salamanders is not the worst thing that could happen to New England or the world.

But, as is often the case in such situations, there is a greater message in the plight of this obscure amphibian. For one thing, salamanders, like birds, are indicator species. When they begin to disappear for no clear reason it is a sign that some broader ecological upset is at work in the community. For another, it has been calculated that the biomass of salamanders in a given tract of woodland in the Northeast probably exceeds that of birds. The blue-spot, in other words, is not such an insignificant creature. In fact, viewed from the long perspective of geologic time, the blue-spot must rate as one of the more successful inventions of evolution.

The ancestral form of the blue-spotted salamander developed sometime during the Carboniferous period, some 350 million years ago. In its time on this earth, it has survived the upwelling of continents, periods of intense volcanic activity, innumerable glacial advances and retreats, a 12-million-year drought, whatever it was that killed the dinosaurs, and any number of similarly cataclysmic events. It is certainly a testimony to the insidious effects of that relative latecomer, *Homo sapiens*, that the blue-spot may not survive the rain that once gave it life.

May/June 1982

The Art of Seeing

She was, at the time, 75, maybe 80 years old, and still living at the cutting edge. Nothing could stop her—heart attacks, the death of friends, the death of lovers, the ruination of the natural world she so loved, the twentieth-century breakdown of society, the physical breakdown of her own body—nothing held her back. Every day before dawn she was off to the woods with any one of the various dogs that she owned in her life, looking at things, plucking things up to look at them more closely, or stepping back to look at them from afar.

There seemed to be nothing in the natural world that she was not interested in—birds, flowers, mosses, algae, rocks, fish, salamanders, and anything else that moved or grew. She was, in short, a member of the old school of naturalist, a species that is sadly in decline in this era of specialization.

From time to time, she and I would go out to a local quarry in search of minerals. It was not the type of place you would expect to find an old lady and a young man together. The road in was rutted and strewn with beer cans and assorted forms of litter. There was an old rain-soaked couch by the entrance to the quarry as well as a number of split mattresses and an abandoned, burned-out car. But she saw only the beauty of the rocks.

As soon as we would step from the car she would streak across the floor of the quarry in her English tweeds and her sensible shoes to clamber up a scree of broken rock at the far end. Halfway up, she would begin picking out rocks, inspecting them closely, and then heaving them down onto the quarry floor to retrieve later. Sometimes she would leave the jumble of rocks and begin to scale the sheer walls in search of finer prizes, holding onto the thin ledges with one hand while she struck off some new chunk of rock with her mineral hammer.

To me, the quarry wall offered nothing more than a blank slate—a confusing jumble of half-broken rocks, sheer faces, drill lines, and deep cracks. But she could see the whole history of the earth there—vast expanses of time, tumultuous volcanic explosions, continental shifts, storms, earthquakes, floods, and extended periods of quiescence. She could also see exquisite, delicate beauty.

All the colors in the world were there, she used to say, all the delicacies of precious stones, and all for free.

She would regress dramatically during these outings. She would become a child again, discovering the world for the first time. Her enthusiasm would mount with each new find, so that by the end of the day she would be seeing marvels in mere flecks of stone. And more often than not, I would see them too; or at least could appreciate her excitement.

It's all a matter of learning to see, she used to tell me. "If only people could see. If only they could learn to really see…."

January 1983

Five Dog Night

ichard Porter of East Charleston, Vermont, aged 79, does not own an electric blanket. He does not have central heat in his three-room cabin, has not heard of modern airtight wood stoves, does not own a kerosene or gas space heater, and regularly allows the fire in his box-type wood stove to burn itself out each night around eleven o'clock. He is not averse to cold drafts and for this reason has never insulated the pine board walls of his cabin even though the temperatures in East Charleston commonly dip below zero degrees Fahrenheit for weeks at a time. And yet, in spite of his apparent lack of conveniences, Porter says he is never cold at night. He has devised a system of living blankets that automatically pile themselves on his bed in response to the temperature.

Porter is the type of mildly eccentric individual who can be found living beyond the confines of the rural towns throughout most of North America. He lives by his wits, working for logging crews whenever he needs money, picking over the local dump for resources he feels need recycling, and getting through the New England winter with as little expenditure of money and energy as possible. Like many who have deserted human society, Porter keeps a number of dogs for companions. Townspeople regularly see him walking along back roads surrounded by his pack, a mixed crew of all sizes and shapes, some large, some small, some friendly, and the rest too lazy to be unfriendly. Because of his companions he has earned for himself the title "The Dog King" among the townspeople. Not surprisingly, it is his subjects who keep him warm at night.

Each winter night about the time the box stove begins to cool, the first of Porter's alternative heating systems—a black and tan hound named Spike—begins to stir from his spot beneath the stove. Spike will climb onto Porter's bed when the room temperature reaches 50 degrees. Louise will get up around 40 degrees. Any colder and the others begin to come in through a dog door that Porter has cut in one of his door panels.

Spike and Louise, his favorites, spend most of their time in the cabin. The

others come in only to sleep, and only when it's cold. They come in a progression, Porter says. Jeff, a collie-like dog with a thick coat, will move in on those nights when the outside temperature reaches 10 degrees and will join the others on the bed shortly thereafter. Alice, a medium-sized dog of indetermined parentage, arrives after the temperature dips below ten. But those nights when the mercury dips below the zero mark the arrival of the warmest dog of all, an immense golden-eyed thing named Bull who has a strong shot of Irish wolfhound in his blood.

Porter says that Bull does not normally appreciate such bourgeois comforts as warm stoves and human companionship. But in his aloof, doglike way, he is as devoted to Porter as any dog of his type could be. Porter believes that it is generally below Bull to come in at night, let alone climb up on the bed with the lesser beings in the pack. But zero-degree nights get the better of the pride and invariably he deserts his usual hideout beneath the porch stairs and squeezes in through the narrow door panel. With Bull on the bed, there is not a night that Porter cannot endure.

Richard Porter has fallen behind the times in some areas of study. He believes, for example, that J. Edgar Hoover would have made a good president, is convinced that the Reagan administration is rife with communists, and was not aware of the fact that this country experienced what was once termed an "energy crisis." On the other hand, he has not been cold at night for 65 years in spite of the fact that he lives in one of the coldest regions in New England and spends no more than one or two hundred dollars a year on energy—mostly for dog food.

December 1983

The Eel Trapper

He ended his days as a parking lot attendant for the beach-going crowds of summer tourists, but in his eyes you could still see the color of the alongshore sea, the brown of the November marsh in his skin. He was a man who had lived entirely from the bounty of the estuary—herring in spring, eels in autumn, clams in summer, scallops and oysters in winter. He was the last trap fisherman in the region, the last commercial eeler and, for at least a decade or two, the oldest yet unretired man in his field. In effect, he was the last of a dying breed of self-sufficient Yankee watermen.

At age 92, with his own demise not far ahead of him, he seemed to draw a sort of energy from the fact that his body and the watery environment he knew best were slipping into dissolution and death at about the same time. As a result he became, in his last years, an ardent environmentalist, lecturing (sometimes ad nauseum) the innocent summer people who came to his parking lot. Given the course of events that had affected him in his life, you could see how he came to such a pass.

There was a time in the 1920s and early 1930s when his fish traps were brimming with life and there was a good market for his catch. But for various reasons his fish-trapping operation began to fail; either the schools moved to another section of the coast, or the fish died, or the market dried up. Furthermore, by the late 1950s and early 1960s, summer boaters—most of them waterskiers and sport fishermen—began to complain about the stakes that he set his nets on. They were too close to the good beaches, they said, and made recreational boating and swimming all but impossible.

So Mr. Benjamin turned to eels and within two years had the largest single eeling operation in the area. He also tapped an excellent market. Around December each year, big buyers would show up from New York City, offer him good cigars, and order more eels than he could possibly catch. "It was for Italians," Mr. Benjamin used to say in his parochial sort of way. "They would eat them at

Christmas, like turkey. But old folks died, and the young ones forgot the good customs and moved away." The market died, and he was left wondering what kind of a world it is in which a tradition that is four or five hundred years old disappears in a single generation.

So he turned, finally, to his old enemies, the tourists. He began selling his eels not for food, but for bait for the fisherman in the bass derbies that were held in his town each autumn. He seemed to regret the change, but he was very old by then, and about the time that he quit fishing yet another threat loomed.

The gossip on the town dock was of diminishing populations of striped bass and, more ominous still, of toxic fish flesh rank with chemicals whose names were so complex they could only be identified by their initials. No one on the docks knew what the letters stood for; they only knew that the chemicals sounded bad and, furthermore, had been informed by greater authorities that they were indeed bad. The chemicals the fishermen couldn't see. The diminished catches were obvious. There was, or would be, less and less need for eel bait.

By this time Mr. Benjamin was working the parking lot, taking tickets and checking beach stickers to make certain that only residents of the community used the beach. He was not very committed to his job, would often let the out-of-towners go for a swim, and would hold up others with his lectures on eels. Eels seemed to be something of a metaphor for him. Through all the wild swings of the fish trade the eel populations had held steady, at least in his area. As long as the elvers showed up in the spring, as long as the adults moved down to the sea, his world could go on.

Then one day he heard of a massive eel kill in a nearby pond; hundreds of adult eel bodies littered the marshes. He grew weak after that, quit his job, and in autumn, by the time eel migration began, he died.

At his age, no one was surprised. He was eulogized in the local papers and the stories spoke of the good long life on the open sea. No one understood what really killed him.

July/August 1984

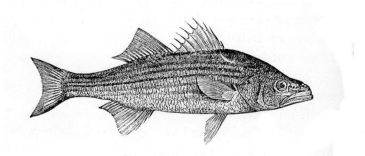

Circle in the Snow

The fact that it was snowing lightly when we set out that day did not matter overly to either of us. My friend was an experienced hiker, having traversed various alpine slopes in Switzerland, and having walked the better part of the Appalachian Trail at one time or another. Furthermore, I knew the region intimately. I had walked through this particular section of the forest almost every day for two years, and in all kinds of weather. The presence of snow only added flavor to the hike.

There were no trails in that section of the state forest, but there were any number of good landmarks—a small ravine with a brook at the bottom, a great gnarled yellow birch, an immense clump of mountain laurel, and, of course, there was the general lay of the land—most of the ridges ran north/south in that part of the world. This was to be a casual walk; we carried no supplies, had no specific goals to attain, and had not bothered to check the weather reports before we went out. There was no need; we planned to be back long before sundown.

By the time we passed the gnarled birch, the sky had darkened considerably, and by the time we left the clump of laurel behind there was a serious snow in progress. We crossed a small valley, climbed to a ridge, tracked along the top for a while, and then, after 40 minutes or so, because of the deepening snow, decided to go back.

I knew my way back well enough. In the beginning we simply followed our own tracks and the ridge lines. But there came a point when, because of the heavy snow, the tracks faded out, and then suddenly the ridges seemed to be running in the wrong direction. I followed them anyway, knowing the navigational anomalies that a whiteout can bring to sailors and bushwackers. In any case, we came to what seemed to be a more sheltered spot where somehow our outward-bound tracks had not yet filled with snow. Knowing they would take us back without regard to other landmarks we simply followed them. We were involved, as I remember, in a discussion of some weighty philosophical matter, not really paying much attention to our situation.

After a half an hour or more it seemed to me that we should have spotted at least one of my usual landmarks. There were many laurel clumps, to be sure, but I couldn't be certain whether any was the large one that I always used as a guide. Furthermore, I had yet to spot the gnarled yellow birch, let alone the sharp ravine with the brook at the bottom. We hiked on anyway, but we began to search for something with a ring of familiarity—something other than white snow and vertical trunks.

After another 15 or 20 minutes I saw a familiar-looking hemlock. A few minutes later, I spotted another signpost, a four-trunked maple, and slowly, one by one, what seemed to be common guideposts began to appear. No matter that they weren't the ones I usually noticed; we had seen them before and were clearly headed in the right direction. Nevertheless the time frames were wrong. We had been hiking for at least an hour, through ever-deepening snow, on the return trip, yet we had only spent 45 minutes at most getting to the turnaround point.

It suddenly occurred to us that there was, perhaps, a remote possibility that we were lost. We rejected the thought immediately. Only white people get lost in the woods; the real earth people, the American Indians, our models in those days, might not know where they were from time to time, but they were never lost. We were in the midst of making this point when my friend saw another familiar hemlock tree. It had a lot more snow on it than the first one we had seen, but then it was snowing a lot harder by that time. We watched for the four-trunked maple, and it appeared right on schedule. Clearly, we were in a rut.

If we had been true Indians we would have had a smoke or made a camp. As it was we kept walking, looking hard now for a break in the circle, and knowing well that to find it we might have to make the entire circuit again, possibly twice—perhaps, my friend suggested, forever. We were still taking all this lightly, probably a good thing in view of the circumstances.

We did indeed go around once. But the second time around I realized that what I was really looking for—the general lay of the land—was impossible to see: the visibility was no more than a few feet. Then about five minutes into the second circuit, we saw what appeared to be a curious channel in the snow, leading off in God knows what direction, but at a definite angle to our vicious circle. The only things that could make such a channel in the snow were two-footed humans or a herd of deer and, since deer have more sense than to travel in such weather, we assumed that the tracks were ours.

It turned out to be a good guess. We got home just past dark after picking our way through an alien landscape of grotesque white shapes. It also turned out to be a record storm for that winter. One more circle and our channel of tracks might have filled, the darkness would have descended, and we would indeed have circled for eternity.

January/February 1985

The Legend of the Golden Fox

The year they saw the golden fox, Mugsy got the contract to clean sticks and driftwood from Boston Harbor. He had a tough, elegant boat named the *Priscilla* and not much to do with her that season, and when he got the contract, in order to celebrate, he decided to hold an Easter egg hunt on the harbor islands.

All this was long ago in the time before there was a Boston Harbor Islands National Recreation Area, in the years when the waterfront was unpolished and nasty, and there were plenty of stories and no lack of storytellers. Mugsy was the outsider. He was a gentleman among wharf rats, a dandy and a dreamer, who never let his aristocratic background, his money, his good looks, and his ritzy friends come between him and the drifters, the boat bums, and the sometime crooks he counted among his best friends. He was a poet manqué, a literate sort who would often shout long quotes from his one great hero, the Sea Rat in *The Wind in the Willows*, while plowing around the harbor in his tug.

"I shipped myself onboard a small trading vessel bound from Constantinople," he would announce to a disparate assemblage of friends and crewmen, "by classic seas whose every wave throbs with a deathless memory, to the Grecian Islands and the Levant. Those were golden days and balmy nights!"

The wharf rats would listen suspiciously. They misunderstood poor Mugsy, but they tolerated him. He was just one more of the various eccentric types who hung around the docks, and a cut above the others at that. It was, after all, Mugsy's friend, Arthur—also a towboat captain—who claimed he liked to hire only murderers because they were loyal. "Thieves you can't trust," he used to say. Mugsy was more discriminating. The wharf rats may have misunderstood him, but they loved his adventures, and on the day of the Easter egg hunt they all piled aboard the *Priscilla* and, under a bright spring sky, steamed toward the islands and Mugsy's previously secreted eggs. There was a street kid on board packing a twenty-two caliber pistol; there were a few sailors, temporarily on the beach; a down-and-out marine painter; and a few of the people who hung around

Estabrook's boatyard. And there was also Serena, Mugsy's companion for that period of his life, an elegant English lady with a refined Oxford accent.

They landed at Peddocks and hunted for eggs, moved on to Georges and Lovells and hunted some more, and then, the eggs depleted, they sailed outbound toward the Brewsters. "Thence we turned and coasted up the Adriatic, its shores swimming in an atmosphere of amber, rose, and aquamarine," said Mugsy, still quoting. Someone broke open one of Mugsy's precious bottles of 1959 Chateau Mouton. And someone else emptied it before they reached the outer islands.

Just off Greater Brewster Mugsy hove to and let the *Priscilla* idle in the swell. Serena went ashore to look around, and when she came back she was in shock. "I've seen a fox," she said. "A magnificent golden fox."

The younger ones streamed ashore, Serena in the lead, while Mugsy kept his vessel off the rocks. They climbed over bedrock and tunneled through brush to the fox's den. The kid with the gun was there, the marine painter, and the Eastabrook crowd. None believed in Serena's fox, and yet as soon as they arrived at the den it poked its head up from between the rocks, scrambled to the top of a rock pile, and halted on the rise, its golden fur flowing in the sea wind.

"A real fox," shouted the kid with the gun. "Helloo foxy," called Serena. "I knew you were here." The fox looked down at the assembled band and fled over the hill, more in horror than in fear.

The kid lost control and, firing madly into the air, dashed over the hill. Back on the *Priscilla*, Mugsy, who heard the shots whistle, signaled desperately for his crew to return. There was chaos and shouting. They chased the kid, caught him, and confiscated his gun, and then, still in awe of the beautiful vision beyond the squalor of the docks, returned to the *Priscilla*. It was the last anyone saw of the golden fox.

Back on board they told and retold the adventure, broke out more wine, and then steamed back to port.

Mugsy was somewhat subdued. "For now I had done with islands for the time," he quoted softly.

Things went downhill after that. At the end of the summer the man with the murderous crew got the cleanup contract. Mugsy borrowed money he couldn't repay, and that winter he disappeared to South America, never to return. The wharf rats missed him. They often talked about his Easter adventure, and even those who missed the event had visions of the golden fox, of something beautiful and good in the harbor beyond the city.

July/August 1986

Why They Seek Light

My father had a soft spot in his heart for fireflies.

We used to spend summers at a rambling nineteenth-century summer house known as the Reed's Creek place, which belonged to some member of my generally extended family. The house was set in a grove of cedars and was surrounded by hayfields, which rolled down to a wide creek where my family kept a number of small boats and a splintery swimming dock. Often in evening, after sunset, my father would retire to the wide porch on the western side of the house and sit there, rocking and watching the hayfields fade from view. The first spark of light from the rising fireflies would inevitably inspire him to launch into some long firefly reminiscence, which his children, his family, and his visiting friends had no doubt heard before.

Part of my father's love of fireflies probably came from his interest in the Orient. He lived in China for three years and would regularly visit Japan during his vacations. While he was there, or perhaps even before he went out to the East, he began reading Lafcadio Hearn, the then-well-known essayist and interpreter of Asian culture. Hearn was a folklorist, among other things, and something of a naturalist, and he had collected a number of essays on the rich insect folklore of Japan. Although my father grew up with hayfields and fireflies, I suspect that part of his appreciation for these insects came from his readings as well as his firsthand experience.

I don't remember much of the lore or reminiscences that my father would spin out on those long summer evenings, but there was one story in particular that stands out because it seemed to explain to me the logical way in which the world is put together. Periodically during those summers, in a Japanese folk tale probably lifted from Lafcadio Hearn, my father would recount the story of Princess Firefly.

It seems that centuries past, in the kingdom of the insects, the king of the fireflies and his queen had a beautifully bright daughter who came of age in spring. Her parents wanted her to marry, but she proved a fickle insect and

in spite of the fact that a retinue of marvelous beetles, praying mantises, lacewings, moths, and butterflies came to court her, none met her fancy. As the years passed, her parents—and indeed the whole insect kingdom—grew more anxious. Each spring they would insist that she take a husband, and each spring she would reject the entire entourage. Finally, in order to please her parents and hold off the suitors, she announced that she would marry the insect who could match her own brilliant light.

One after another the brave suitors took up the challenge. The great bronzed Junebug flew off into the darkness, seeking light. Hopeful moths fluttered through the night, lacewings and crane flies and even tiny gnats circled through the dark world hoping to steal fire to bring back to the glorious princess. In time the suitors found light in the tiny flickering oil lamps of country people. They clustered around the fire, circled it, or landed nearby and watched, waiting. Periodically one of them would dash into the flame to try to catch the fire, only to singe his wings and fall struggling to the base of the lamp. Try as they might, not one was ever able to bring back the fire, nor match the brilliance of Princess Firefly, and in a curious twist of traditional folklore, she never married and lived happily ever after as a dowager queen. But the poor suitors have never given up, and to this day they can still be seen, flitting and circling in the dark night, battering themselves against lamps, ever hopeful after all these centuries.

There was always a silence after my father completed his tale. Beyond the porch, the river turned black. No one spoke. There was only the sound of the rockers on the old wood porch floor, the *jug o'rum* of the bullfrog chorus from the pond behind the main house, the *quock* of night-herons down on the dark riverbank, the sultry air, and below the house, like Japanese lanterns, the dancing of the lights of ten thousand fireflies.

May/June 1988

Cape Calamity

It was evening on Route 28. It was also 1963, and fore and aft of us, low-slung Fords and Buicks were steaming by under the influence of hot drivers with close-cropped hair and high-rolled T-shirts, some with cigarette packs tucked in the sleeves. My older brother and I had been making a boat delivery, and we had been offshore for three days straight. My brother, who had wrung more saltwater out of his socks than most people have sailed over, was getting upset. The exhaust and the roadside hamburger stands were getting to him. His car had lost a number of critical parts and was unable to maintain a proper speed, and the drivers of the big Buicks were getting angry. One after another they would charge up behind us, tailgate for an improper period, and then pass. All we were doing was attempting to get to Boston alive.

In exasperation we pulled over. My brother stood sadly by the side of the road, shaking his head.

"What's up?" I asked him.

"Just look," he said. He was staring at one of the roadside stands that were a common element of the landscape in those unfortunate years. It was an ice cream stand that advertised itself with an immense, towering model of a milk bottle, one of the definitive landmarks on that section of Route 28 in those spicy bygone days.

We looked up and down the highway. As far as the eye could see, there were similar, though less ambitious, stands lining the road. Little crowds of dusty Bucks had gathered around them, like cows at a trough.

"What's the matter?" I asked again.

"This has got to be the ugliest spot in all America," he said.

Indeed.

But Cape Cod was a sad land from the beginning, the soil poor, the trees half-stunted, storms forever sweeping landward, tearing up the coast and spraying saltwater across the whole peninsula. It was a hard land. Even the Wampanoags had a hard time there, and to make things worse, after Europeans arrived in their winged ships, the plagues came with them and laid waste to the meager villages.

Perhaps it was prelude. Even William Bradford found the place grim. The world stood before his pilgrims with a weather-beaten face, the whole country full of woods and thickets with a wild and savage hue, a hideous desolate wilderness filled with wild beasts and wild men, and only the ocean behind them, "…a main bar and gulf to separate them from all the civil parts of the world," as Bradford wrote.

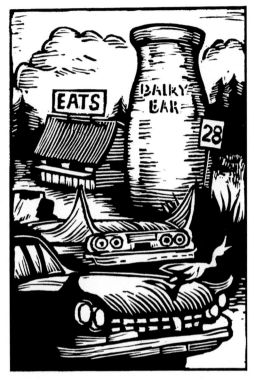

"Better than it used to be." I said to my brother. "At least we can eat in winter."

He looked at me as if I were crazy. He is eight years older than I am, and he sometimes reminds me of Captain Ahab. I stared back, as I sometimes would with him, and he quoted *Moby Dick*, as he sometimes would. "Unfix thine eye," he spit, echoing Ahab. "More intolerable than fiend's glarings is a doltish stare."

We drove on. It was indeed ugly. And as it was a Sunday evening in the summer, it was indeed crowded. We got stuck near Buttermilk Bay.

He began to rant again. Three days at sea never did my brother much good. It only made him worse.

On the other hand, maybe he was right. Two hundred years after William Bradford arrived, the Cape had not fared much better. The scrawny forest of oak and pitch pine and beech had been stripped, the fauna had been extirpated,

and the houses were small and roughly built. Henry Thoreau, passing through on a walking tour in 1850, claimed that the residents of Chatham had to use fog for shade instead of trees. He said the farmers were so unfamiliar with trees that they would refer to them by the personal pronoun, "I got him out of the woods," one old farmer told Thoreau. "He doesn't bear well," he said of another.

The people were poor and had bad teeth. They built fences from ships' ribs, scavenged from the wrecks, of which there were many. It used to be said that if all the wrecks that piled up on the back side of the Cape were laid bow to stern, they would make a solid wall from Chatham to Provincetown.

"Things are getting better," I told my brother in 1963.

"Just wait," he said.

July/August 1988

The Copper Beech

Sometimes on warm summer nights a breeze would come up, and you could hear the whispers of the things that lived in the leaves of the upper branches of the beech tree. Often I could see their quick forms moving in the darker shadows, and once one looked at me directly; I saw its large round eyes and its skinny hands.

For years a wolf lived in that tree. My older brothers had seen him on many occasions. He was strong and could jump from the upper limbs to the bedroom where I slept, but he left the year I turned seven, the same year the tree-dwelling things moved in. Probably they drove him out.

We would always climb the copper beech during the day in summer. The bark of the high, ancient trunk was smooth and cool; there was always a breeze at the top, and there were many curving branches to lie along. Sometimes we turned into leopards while we were there. We would growl deeply and watch for baboons crossing the open ground between the watering hole and the great rocky cliff where they lived. The tree dwellers were nowhere to be seen during the day. They retreated into the trunk and came out only at night; in winter they would move underground.

Autumn was a tragic season for the copper beech. One by one, without the flare of the other trees in my yard, the leaves disappeared, and our nest and lair would be revealed. The baboons went south. Sometimes during high winds, the wolf came back. You could hear him whining, my brothers said. I listened, but I was ten, and it really was only the wind. In spring the furry aphids would appear. They covered the branches and squished against our fingers as we climbed. We would go up early in the season, just before the buds were swelling, and we climbed higher than at any time of year. The tip of the tree was spidery and swayed with our weight, bringing us earthward from a thousand feet. We wedged ourselves in the crooks and surveyed the town—the high roofs, and the trees, higher than the houses, and the yards below, dark and green, and worth finding out about.

The town where the copper beech grew was old, a product of the midnineteenth century, and I began to notice that in other yards there were other copper beeches. These too we climbed; there were no things living in the leaves, and there were no wolves, but the trees made a pleasant landscape, a darkness in the green light of summer, an autumnal Victorian gloom that I came to appreciate for its mystery. I ranged beyond my yard, and counted copper beeches.

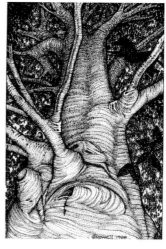

By the time I was twelve, I knew all the beeches in town. From my perch I could count no fewer than five, three to the north in a wide, landscaped property owned by the notorious Mrs. MacKay who dressed always in Chinese silks and had a Scottish gardener who chased us whenever we scaled his trees. To the west, near the center of town, there was an immense tree, the queen of all the beeches. It grew in front of a tearoom in a yard surrounded by a wrought-iron fence with cruel fleur-de-lis-shaped spikes. This tree we never climbed; we watched it from afar, in admiration. It absorbed all light—a deep, penumbral silence reigned in the interior of its canopy. Things lived in it.

But the town was changing. The tearoom closed, the tree dwellers disappeared from the beech in my side yard. My older brothers grew up, and one day men came with chain saws and cut down the beech in front of the tearoom.

A furniture store moved in, and where the tree once stood, the owner put up a sign advertising chairs. My family was upset. We would close our eyes when we drove by, pretending it hadn't happened. One night I wrote a letter in ink. "It took a hundred years to grow," I wrote to the owner. "Where will you be in a hundred years?"

It didn't bring the tree back, and, in any case, I was fourteen by then. The wolf was memory, the things that whispered in the leaves on summer nights had retreated to the deeper woods, and I never again saw their dark round eyes and their bony clasping fingers.

October 1988

Peace in Our Time

osemary Little lived out in the country. She grew apples and pears in a quiet little dooryard garden and made jams and jellies each year in autumn. In summer she ate eggplants and tomatoes, spiced with basil, and whenever September would roll in, she would dig and spade and wait for the hummingbirds to appear in her flower gardens. She lived a quiet life without praise or blame, managing her days more by the natural cycles of the seasons than by tedious human schedules. She swam all summer. She gathered mushrooms in autumn after the rains; she watched the leaves turn, and she felt lonely in November after they had fallen. When December came she would make tea in the afternoon and stay indoors, watching the grim weather. She had no television. "The programs make me sad," she used to say.

Once, years back, she worked in the city in a bureau that dealt with environmental issues, but that too made her sad. "The news was always dark. There were polluters at every bend. There were developments destroying everyone's backyard. There were actual criminals." And then there was the world at large. "The greenhouse effect. Polluted air, polluted seas, polluted groundwater— everything polluted and dying. The world sick."

She quit and moved away from the city.

For a while she supported herself by working in a garden center. After a single year in that place, removed from development and news, she began to notice that there was an actual order to the world. Birds came back each year in spring. In the woodlands on rainy nights in April, she would see salamanders. She would hear frogs calling.

She knew where all the woodland wildflowers grew—the lovely arbutus and the spring beauties, the bloodroot and the crinkleroot, and the lacy little Dutchman's breeches. She loved them all; she learned all the seasons of flowering and knew that Mayapples meant the end. "After them the woods leafed out in lace. But I never minded. It was time to garden."

She grew lettuce and asparagus, peas and beans, cosmos and marigolds, and summerlong she watched for her specialties, her eggplants and her tomatoes. She swam at the local lake—the first to dip into the chill waters of June, the last to swim in September in the time of pears, when the water was chilled again and fresh. She warmed herself with apple pies and quiet dinner parties where people entertained themselves with small talk and never mentioned criminals. She practiced her cello at night and, in the mornings, speculated on things that did not matter. How many thousands of nuts buried by squirrels in the forest are actually retrieved by squirrels? How many of those unretrieved nuts actually sprout? How much of the northern hardwood forest was planted by squirrels?

"Maybe these things are important," she said.

Rosemary Little lived out in the country and after three years learned once again to enjoy her life. She used to think the world was black. She used to think the bomb was inevitable. She used to think the glaciers were melting.

"Maybe it's all true," she said. "But here is what I think now. Life is a series of small moments of grace in the midst of an otherwise indifferent universe. Go tell that to your readers."

December 1988

The Tree of Life

The Kiwai of New Guinea, like many preliterate groups, have a great respect for trees. In the late nineteenth century, when they were first given iron axes by the British, they were reluctant to use them; there were certain trees in particular that they refused to cut down. They believed, it was learned, that trees were inhabited by *etengena*, or spirit beings who were somehow connected with the soul of the tree. Before any tree could be felled, the axman would have to request that the *etengena* move to another tree, and if his arms felt heavy while cutting, or if the work seemed particularly hard, it was a clear sign that the *etengena* had not yet deserted the tree, and it was perhaps best left standing.

The Kiwai were not alone in their reverence for trees. Closer to home, our own European ancestors practiced various forms of tree worship, the best-known example of which is perhaps the religion of the Druids, who so revered the ancient oaks of the British Isles. But there were also sacred groves in what is now Uppsala in Sweden. The Slavs maintained holy forests where no tree could be cut; there were sacred groves throughout pre-Christian Germany, and perhaps most significant of all, according to Norse mythology, the very pivot of the earth was the Yggdrasil, the world ash. Its limbs spread over the world and stood above the heavens, and its roots penetrated into the abyss of hell.

Tree worship endured in Europe until the fourteenth century. The Lithuanians, the last converted to Christianity, had sacred groves around their villages; it was considered a sin to so much as break a twig from one of the trees there.

It is little wonder that trees and forests play such an important role in the spiritual life of pre-Christian Europe. In Roman times, all of Britain was forested; Germany was blanketed with dark, impenetrable woods; northern Italy was treed with chestnuts, elms, and oaks; and the dark and fearsome Ciminian Forest rolled south along the Italian peninsula all the way to Rome. Even the stark, light-flooded hills of Greece were once treed with oak and pine, although as early as the fifth century BCE Plato lamented the deforestation of the archipelago. Nor was Europe alone; in fact, until some ten thousand years ago, when agriculture began

to take hold as a way of life, most of the earth was covered with a green sheltering mantle of trees. It is estimated that there were 15 or 16 billion acres of woods on the planet. Less than one-third of the great overarching forest remains.

But quite apart from the fact that the human race must have grown up under the shade of the tree, there is something innately nurturing or good or beautiful about trees. There is no way that our prescientific ancestors could have known in a rational way, but trees and the existence of higher forms of life on this planet are inextricably connected.

A single, good-sized maple may contain several thousand green leaves, which can expose some two thousand square yards—about half an acre—to the sky and the sun. These leaves take carbon dioxide from the air and hydrogen from the waters of the soil, combine the two with sunlight, and produce carbohydrates, which are capable of sustaining other forms of life. A growing tree uses carbon dioxide at a rate of about forty-eight pounds per year, which comes to about ten tons for every acre of forest. Every ton of new wood extracts about one and a half tons of carbon dioxide and produces in return a little more than a ton of oxygen. If you consider that there are still about ten billion acres of forest on earth, that means that some one hundred billion tons of carbon dioxide are being used up each year by the forests of the world.

Carbon dioxide has become a problem in our time. Because of the destruction of the world forest, because of the human use of fossil fuels and the increase in other gases associated with industrial activity, the dynamics of the earth's atmosphere and its plant life are changing, and there is now too much carbon dioxide in the earth's atmosphere. The result is a phenomenon popularly known as the greenhouse effect.

But as is often the case in world events, it is perhaps important to relearn what was known by our forebears. Trees are life, more than we may know, and as the Kiwai made clear, we should perhaps be more careful when we go into the forest.

September 1989

A Certain Slant of Light

Each December, about the time that the last of the milkweed pods crack in the old fields across from my house, I begin to see white-throated sparrows around here. I know then that sometime during that same week the last phoebes will leave, and I'll see a few lingering thrushes, and the sad little flights of sparrow flocks will become increasingly evident.

It is also about that same time of year that I begin to notice a silvery, raking light spearing through the bare limbs of the large trees in the older sections of the town. The grass will still be green on lawns, the privet hedges will still hold their leaves, and, in the woods, the oaks and the beeches will cling desperately to the last remnants of a forgotten summer.

For years I used to keep a record of little events of this sort. I would begin in late winter and follow the slow opening of the season through the spring and into summer, and on into fall, winter, and then back to early spring. Each year, around the middle of June, after the indigo buntings and the kingbirds arrived, the entries would become sporadic. I would record a few flowerings of the field wildflowers, the first calling of the bullfrogs from the pond below my house, but then by midsummer the journals would dry up altogether, only to begin again in autumn, about the time that the monarch butterflies would appear and the little migratory hummingbirds would start to show up in my flower gardens. After that I would record the changing leaves, the last of the oaks, then another slump, then the first ice, then the first snow, the appearance of Orion, and the coming of the juncos and the winter finches.

For three or four years I kept at it, and each year I began to fill in a little more so that the blank periods would take shape as well. And then I began to get interested in endings as well as beginnings. When did the last dandelion bloom? When did the snowy tree crickets stop chirping? When did the meadow crickets give up? (Surprisingly late in November it turned out.) Finally, three or four years after I filled out the whole year, I began to notice a phenomenon. Every year the same events would occur on almost exactly the same date.

After a while I stopped keeping records. Almost incidentally, without trying, I found I had committed the year to memory. I threw away the calendars and began marking time by nature, so that when I first saw the phoebe on my land in spring I would know it was March 27. The forsythia would bloom, the grass would turn green, and I would know that it was April 10. The wild plums would bloom on April 22. The first lightning bugs would appear in the meadow behind my house on July 9. By August 27 the nighthawks would appear in the evening sky and so on throughout the summer and fall until the fifth of December.

Toward late afternoon on that day, somewhere between Lincoln, where I work, and Littleton, where I live, I would notice that the shadows cast by the old oak trees had lengthened dramatically, and I would see in the west that peculiar slant of silvery light, and I would know that the dreaded month had finally arrived, with all its baggage of endings, its hope, its innuendos of things to come, and its remembrances of things gone by.

There should be nothing unusual in all of this. It is the way people have marked time for the better part of human history. But in an age when the great circle of the year is cut into snippets, when response is measured in nanoseconds and time itself has been analyzed into nothingness, natural time seems barbarically inaccurate and, for this very reason, worth reviving.

December 1990

Living Well is the Best Revenge

In the mid-1980s, using locally cut timber and a few borrowed tools, I built a small one-room cabin in a hickory grove and spent a year living as close as I could to the natural world. I had no electricity, no running water, and I heated the cottage with wood, at least some of it garnered from land that belonged to me.

One February night while I was in the cottage, there was a terrific snowstorm, followed by high winds and a bitter cold snap. I learned the next morning that the town and its associated industries were in chaos. The power had been off for twelve hours or more. Computer companies had lost all their backup. Traffic was stalled and snarled, and people at home were shivering in the dark. All I knew of this was that the wind had made beautiful patterns in the snow at the edge of the meadow beside my cottage.

A year in the woods observing the natural world is hardly innovative ground; I was taking my cues, of course, from Henry Thoreau. And during the time that I lived there, in order to better understand the roots of my experiment, I read or reread Thoreau's writings, including the better part of his journals. The more I read, the more I understood how prescient this Mr. Henry Thoreau really was. So many of his observations and pronouncements have proved true, and so many of the issues that he concerned himself with have come around to haunt us in our time, not the least of which is the main one, namely the way we go about making a living.

Thoreau says he went to Walden to drive life into a corner and find out what his necessities were. He did away with nonessentials, borrowed an axe, cut some timber, bartered a few bricks, and built his one-room cabin by Walden Pond. For a while he cooked outdoors; he didn't even have a fireplace until December, and he would commonly let the fire die even on the coldest winter nights.

He gives a careful accounting of his annual income and expenses in *Walden*, down to the three cents for a watermelon, and the six cents he spent on a pumpkin. All told, he calculates that he expended no more than eight dollars and seventy-four cents on food that year, less on clothing, and even less on

what we would now term energy costs, i.e., two dollars for lamp oil. His firewood was free; he scavenged it from the woods. The construction of the house was his big expense, twenty-eight dollars and twelve cents.

His example was purposely extreme. He wanted to demonstrate that one could distill life to its essence and continue to live well, not only well, but ecstatically in his case. Given the fact that, throughout the literate world, at both a scholarly and popular level, we are still discussing his philosophy (if not practicing it), it is safe to say that Thoreau succeeded in making his point.

One of Thoreau's disciples, Mahatma Gandhi, not only successfully put into practice the Thoreauvian concept of civil disobedience, but also attempted to spread the idea of a simplified economy. Gandhi promoted the Thoreauvian view that the essence of civilization is not the multiplication of wants but the elimination of need. It is a message that—in spite of dwindling global resources, the increasing gulf between the rich and the poor, the continued erosion of the environment, and the drastic loss of species diversity—has yet to be accepted by decision makers.

The lesson predates Thoreau and Gandhi, however. In fact it predates civilization. The words ecology and economics have the same root, *oikos*, the house, and the basic principles of each field—that is, the orderly arrangement and management of affairs of the house—are in fact interchangeable. Earth is our house, and any successful economic system should be able to manage the house in an orderly manner. Any other system is unworkable in the end.

January/February 1992

Return of the Native

One still autumn night some years ago, I was out in the woods under a smoky half moon when I heard a wolf howl. I had just climbed a ridge and was resting on a stone wall with a darkened, grassy meadow ahead of me and the deep, mysterious hollows of the woods behind. The howl sounded out from the area that I had just come through. It was a long, brassy yowl that began with a series of short barks and rose in a classical wolfly crescendo, and it was repeated several times, growing fainter with each howl.

I would wager that nobody raised in a European cultural tradition hears such a sound without hearing as well the full scope of wolf mythology. I shuddered. Then I returned to reason. Wolves don't attack people, and in any case this was eastern Massachusetts, and the last wolves were extirpated from this valley by 1723, according to the local histories. What I had heard, of course, was an eastern coyote. I later learned that a lone male coyote will sometimes howl like a wolf when it is not traveling with a pack. I was not at all surprised to hear this. In fact, I had been waiting for them.

Because of a variety of historical accidents, the land around the house in which I live has yet to be developed. There is a series of old fields that drop down to the wide floodplain of a slow-moving brook, and there are three working farms to the north and west and nearly a square mile of woodland. There are foxes, muskrats, otters, raccoons, opossums, and far too many skunks. It was only a question of time before a coyote showed up.

Eastern coyotes, whoever they are, wherever they came from, have been increasing in number in New England for over forty years. Records indicate that they were in the Adirondack region in the 1940s and by the late 1950s had made it to Massachusetts. One was seen in Otis in the midfifties and a year later one turned up at Quabbin.

Whether these are a new breed of coyote recently arrived, or a return of the native, is a matter of debate among mammalogists. But all agree that a large canid of some sort was living here when the first English settlers arrived and that, in keeping with European tradition, the thing, whatever it was, had to be destroyed.

At first the colonists tried bounties using the local Indians as hunters and paying as much as ten shillings or a bushel of corn for the head of a wolf. Fittingly perhaps, given the Judeo-Christian culture of the colonists, the façade of an early church north of Boston was adorned with wolf heads. But once having cleared the wolves from settled regions, the Indians ranged the forest and brought in wolf heads from elsewhere. They also tried selling the same wolf head twice, until the colonists started cutting ears. The Europeans tried dog packs to hunt the wolves, then baits and poisons, and guns on trip wires, and then, finally, they got the right idea and began cutting swamps and "waest grownds" that sheltered the wolf packs, a tradition that is still continuing to this day for different reasons!

The current thinking is that the coyote we see and hear in the backyards of suburban New England does indeed have some wolf genes, picked up as the existing western coyote population moved eastward through the wilderness of the Great Lakes region and Canada. Now coyotes are found everywhere. Individuals have made it across the Cape Cod Canal and have been sighted on the lower Cape; they appear within Route 128; one was seen on Marblehead Neck, and of course packs of coyotes are common in the Berkshires and everywhere else throughout rural New England.

This relative of the large canid that killed the livestock of the earliest settlers still has a taste for sheep and chickens and will not refuse a well-fed house cat if it fails to make it to the nearest tree. But this supposedly vicious predator, with its gleaming, yellow eyes, more commonly makes do with mice, frogs, birds, berries, and even corn.

The beauty of all this is that nature abides. The wolf of history, or something very like it, has returned because the primeval New England forest, or something very like it, has returned. The English invaders who settled here in the seventeenth century attempted to remake the New World into a mirror image of the Old World. In fact, they very nearly succeeded. But lurking in the little corners and undisturbed pockets of woodland, primal America endured, and now the ancient order has reasserted itself. Black bears wander into suburban yards in Clinton, herds of white-tailed deer graze at the woodland edges, the beaver floods backyards and streets, and, sometimes at night, in the middle of a civilized sleep, the wolf howls outside the bedroom window.

March/April 1992

View from the Bridge

The finest hour of my career took place at 5:30 p.m., November 9, 1965, in the middle of the George Washington Bridge. I was in school in New York City at the time, and I used to commute from New Jersey on a bicycle. I had calculated that, give or take a few minutes, the bicycle was about as fast as public transportation or the automobile, sometimes faster, and, unlike the car, was good for your health, did not pollute, and would outlast an automobile by many years, without much care. This was considered a peculiar stand in those innocent years of boundless energy reserves and open frontiers, but I persevered.

On the evening of November 9, emerging from a late class, I observed an unusual phenomenon for New York City, the orange half-moon rising between the darkened buildings of the college. It took me a while to realize that the reason I could see the moon was that the electricity was off. I thought something had gone wrong with the power on campus until I ventured into the streets—they too were dark. The city was strangely silent; I could hear the shuffle of footsteps on the sidewalk and the mumble of hushed conversation, and here and there candlelight glimmered in a few restaurant windows. At one point on the street, I came upon a long, silent line of downcast commuters emerging from the stalled subway.

Rumors began to spread: the power outage was citywide; it was the work of saboteurs, of communists. Someone said they heard that the whole East Coast was without electricity, but that was too outrageous to be believed.

I got on my bicycle and started home through the darkened streets. People were standing about in little groups, and I noticed that they were actually talking to one another. Cars and buses were jammed up and barely moving because the stoplights weren't working. I rode past street after street of stalled traffic and out onto the bridge. Below me I could see the black river, the great autumnal moon floating over the dark island of the city. Halfway over, it struck me that the New Jersey side of the river was dark as well. I got off my bicycle and looked north and south. As far as I could see there was only the primordial Hudson, with the dimmed heights of the Palisades to the west, open water of the harbor to the south, and, behind me, the unreal city. I am sorry to have to report that I felt vindicated.

I've had other moments of satisfaction since that time. I am one of the perverse individuals who actually enjoyed the long gas lines during the so-called energy crisis of 1974 and '75. In my opinion, things got better for a while back then. People started taking account of where energy came from, and, for a few months, maybe even a year, it looked as if this crisis-oriented society would finally start to formulate some sort of a sensible, energy-efficient transportation system.

It didn't happen of course. The 1980s make up in manifold for what still small voice of reason was uttered in the mid-1970s. But even so, now in the 1990s, there are glimmerings of hope. It did not take a massive blackout, nor an energy crisis, nor a war for oil supply, to convince thinking scientists that total reliance on oil and coal was an endgame. Efficient systems such as magnetic levitation trains, high-speed rail, electric vehicles, alternative fuels, flexible fuel vehicles, fuel cells, and any number of similar innovations have been available for two decades. But in the past, sound transportation planning in this country has come up against a massive, centralized power structure known as Detroit, which is opposed to anything but huge, consumptive, gasoline-powered, high-speed, inhumane vehicles that waste energy, pollute the air, annihilate wildlife and people, and have been single-handedly responsible for the destruction of urban centers, the creation of a vast, sprawling, indifferent suburbia, and the ruination of the American landscape.

Now Detroit is foundering, and, rather than blame the Japanese, it would perhaps be more constructive to fall back on the old American idea of self-reliance and design a sustainable and humane transportation system.

May/June 1992

Sundays in the Sky

From the meadow in which I am now lying, I can see a mere slice of sky between the surrounding trees. It is clear, warm, also September, and a northwest wind is ringing down high, fair-weather clouds that sail along the ridge like tall ships and cross above me. A late night has sapped me of all ambition, so instead of working in the garden, as I had intended, I lie on my back in the grass to rest a while, perhaps to sleep. But there is too much happening.

A few yards above me green darner dragonflies dart by, the meadow crickets are singing madly in the surrounding fields, and the little red dragonflies in the genus *Sympetrum* land here and there beside me, zoom off on a mission, and then return to land. I alternately doze and wake and watch the sky.

I am staring into an ill-defined, infinite atmosphere, a space of nothingness where the air is bell clear. But, in the space of a few minutes, things float, wing, drift, or fly by: a broad-winged hawk, a tuft of milkweed, crows, something dark and fast (probably a dragonfly), a slow-flying wasp, its legs dangling more fluff, and ever and always the great parade of clouds.

Hamlet saw camels in the clouds, then weasels, then a whale. English painter John Constable saw brooding skyscapes, Fragonard saw porcelain, Turner saw fire and conflagration. N.C. Wyeth saw a great sky giant passing in the thunderheads beyond the shores of the Atlantic beaches. All I see today is a dog's head, first a spaniel, blunt nosed, with a rounded forehead, then something with a longer nose, then something very like a Doberman.

Just as the Doberman's head breaks up, I see tiny specks against the white cloud. I know better than to let specks drift by on a September day, so I rouse myself, go in the house, and return with binoculars. There, overhead, descending now in a long stretched-out line, are ten or twenty hawks, probably broad-wings, drifting out of a gyre.

Crows call. I watch a flight shift from the white pines on the top of the ridge to the hickories on the southeastern slope. Much excitement among them, much cawing, with bowed heads and beaks. A red balloon, high amidst the blue, slowly proceeds to the southeast, as if on a mission. A plane drones by, headed west, then another, also headed west. One follows a few minutes later, a type known, I believe, as a Tomahawk. (Why do so many small planes and fast cars have to be named for weapons or predatory birds and mammals?, I wonder.)

I used to have a problem with low-flying, noisy planes passing over this meadow on Sunday mornings. I made inquiries and found that in all likelihood it was the work of weekend pilots, flying out to breakfast at various airports west of Boston. After the Tomahawk passes, I try to make a calculation of the amount of energy that must be wasted in these breakfast flights, but I fall asleep before I can even begin to figure anything.

A hawk screams, a real one. A red-tail, headed in the wrong direction—northeast. Spiderlings on gossamer drift past, their lines glistening in the sun. Flies skip just above me, a bee, more fluff, another plane, and then high up, its wings steady and its long neck stretched southward, an impossible vision, an anhinga!

I snatch up the binoculars and look more carefully and have to conclude that this is an exceptionally long-necked cormorant. I fall back. Ten minutes later a flight of some ten to fifteen cormorants drifts by, high against the steady march of clouds.

I am used to these surprises in the sky. Once, lying in the same meadow on a summer evening, watching the bats course overhead, I saw an immense tropical bat materialize out from the dark walls of trees beyond the clearing. It soared above me in a twisting flight, dove, and rose again, and, by the time I realized it was a nighthawk, it was gone.

After lunch I fall into a deep sleep. By midafternoon the great parade is still passing—the hawks, the dragons, the fluff, the slow procession of shiplike clouds. It strikes me that elsewhere in the world this must be one of those autumnal days when watchers of the skies see massive flights of hawks passing down the ridges, so, refreshed from my nap, I drive to a nearby cleared height and spend an hour watching the western sky. Nothing appears, the winds have dropped, the clouds settle into low-lying banks in the west, like distant dunes. I should have stayed home.

That night after dark I went back to the meadow. The fair-weather clouds had dispersed, and the black sky was moonless and clear. Overhead I could see the last of the Summer Triangle, with the great constellation, the Swan, at one angle. Like all good migratory birds, now that autumn had arrived, she had swung her long neck around to the south.

January/February 1993

Saving Graces

I saw another disaster the other day. On Route 117 in Lincoln, just between Farrar Pond and Mount Misery, an innocent painted turtle ventured out onto the road, intent on crossing. Ahead of me, there was a steady stream of oncoming traffic; behind me, an impatient driver in a white Camaro, riding my tail. I saw tragedy in the making and pulled over to rescue the turtle, but the Camaro swerved around me and sped on. He caught the side of the shell and spun the turtle into the opposite lane. The oncoming traffic flattened it.

It was rush hour. People had to get home.

This is the fate of turtles at this time of year. Each spring, starting in April, they venture from ponds where they have spent the winter to lay their eggs in dry, upland soils, often crossing back roads and highways in the process. Turtles have enough problems in late twentieth-century New England even without roads. Six of the dozen formerly common species have declined significantly in number, having fallen victim to loss of wetlands, pollution, pesticides—not to mention indifferent, even vindictive, drivers in high-speed cars. It is not a good age for turtles.

It is not a good age for people. The Carter Center is tracking the course of no fewer than thirty wars and over one hundred serious conflicts. Industrial chemicals are eroding the very structure of the earth's sheltering atmosphere; air pollution is altering the world climate; there are too many people on earth; what food there is is not being distributed equitably; and now the whole course of civilization is conspiring to undo a class of animal that has endured on the planet since the age of the dinosaurs.

In the face of it all, the least one can do is help turtles cross roads.

Here in eastern New England, where there are a lot of ponds and wetlands and, in certain areas, a healthy local population of turtles, that is no small task. On certain days in late May I sometimes have to stop two or three times. The setting is always the same. Ahead on the road, when you are least expecting it, you see a thing very like a rock. Come closer and you will see the shell, the head extended, those beady, seemingly intelligent eyes cautiously regarding the passing cars. Sometimes they make a dash for it (or as much of a dash as a turtle is capable of). Sometimes they forge on in the face of certain dissolution. Rarely have I seen one turn back.

I pull over and wave off traffic. Around me the indifferent drivers wail by, rushing to God knows where. Some swerve away perilously, some brake, some even pull over, but most stream past without altering their course. Too often I am too late and have to witness the violence of the roads, the dreaded impact, the spin of the shell, perhaps a second strike. Sometimes, though, I am able to carry the potential victim across and set it on course.

My favorites are the big snappers, the ones who detest rescue. I love to see them stand off cars, glaring. I love the way they rise up, hissing and lunging when you come near. I like the way they attempt to kill you even when you've got them by the tail and they must know, or believe at least, that their end has come.

I have learned a great deal in the years of turtle salvage. I have learned that it is fruitless to turn them back from their destinations. They will simply try again after you leave. I have also learned that suburban women in high heels and jewelry are not necessarily terrified of huge snapping turtles. I once came across a group of properly attired ladies on a back road in Carlisle wheeling an immense, gape-jawed snapper to safety in a wheelbarrow. I have learned that at least 50 percent of American drivers are not watching the road. I have seen them run over turtles without pause. I have learned never to prejudge fast drivers in late-model muscle cars.

Once, on a narrow back road, I was tailgated by such a car for miles. I could see the driver in the rear-view mirror—he was hunched over the wheel, his head tilted to one side impatiently, wraparound dark glasses, wide, angry mustache. And then ahead, around a sharp curve, too late to stop short because of the tailgater, I saw a turtle, a spotted, a once-common species. I swerved past and pulled over, certain that the speeder would strike, probably out of spite. I heard a squeal of brakes, and before I could even get out of the car he was there, cradling the turtle in his hands. He carried it across the road and let it go in a marsh. "Spotted turtle," he said to me when I arrived on the scene. "These are rare. We've got to take care of these guys."

May/June 1993

Time and the River

I once knew an eighty-year-old man whose passion was Sung Dynasty vases and whose choice of exercise was kayaking on the Concord River. Over the years he came to know the river intimately; he knew the quiet coves that the wood ducks favored and where to find the best pickerelweed beds. He also knew the location of a submerged stone wall just downstream from the North Bridge.

One quiet summer evening while he was out in his kayak, a high-speed powerboat, trailing a huge wake, sped by and swamped him. By way of revenge, the old man lured the offending vessel aground on the submerged wall, destroying the engine in the process.

The event is telling. In an age of cyberspace and cigarette boats, one wonders whether the art of knowing the waters, of intimacy with a river, is now the sole province of old people in kayaks and canoes. Time and running water seem inextricably bound, and in order to understand the meaning, to read the metaphors, it is possible that you have to have aged. World literature is filled with examples. Mark Twain wrote *Life on the Mississippi*, his account of the river he knew as a boy, when he was in his fifties. A year later, having got the particulars down, so to speak, he wrote the American classic *Huckleberry Finn*. Joseph Conrad had to retire from the sea before he could assemble *Heart of Darkness* from journal notes he had made years before on the Congo River. Norman Maclean wrote *A River Runs Through It* when he was in his seventies, haunted throughout his life, as he says, by the waters of the Big Blackfoot River, which he had known as a child. Edwin Way Teale saved his long-planned book about the Sudbury River, *A Conscious Stillness*, for the end, and in fact waited too long. He died while he was writing it.

A river, no matter how large or small, is really not any one thing. It is a compilation of waters, and the waters are compilations of lands, of hill brooks, of dells, swamps, upland marshes, forests, bogs, and those mossy little sinks you come across on mountaintops where wood frogs and toads seem to congregate. The essence is not what you see; it lies somewhere in the surrounding hills, between waters and sky, between the narrow summer banks and the wide flooded shores of spring. And the meaning of river, in the larger sense, is obscure at best. You have to have lived through a series of years in one place to know that.

Henry Thoreau, who somehow assumed some of the wisdom of age before he died at forty-four, says if you can know the local waters you can know the universe. He ranked the poor "much abused Concord River" with the great rivers of the world, the Mississippi, the Ganges, the Nile. He saw the river as a constant lure to distant enterprise and adventure, an invitation to explore the interior of continents. Dwellers at headwaters would naturally be inclined to follow the trail of their waters to see the "end of the matter." He was thinking of earthly territory, of course, and the sea, but as always with Thoreau, he was also thinking of the great transcendental metaphors that are embodied in the natural world. "What a piece of wonder a river is," he wrote.

It is the natural conclusion for anyone who takes the idea of river to "the uttermost ends of the earth," as Conrad phrased it. But in the end it may not necessarily be age that allows insight. I once knew a little boy who from an early age had a natural fascination with running water. One day, standing on a bridge above the roaring waters of a brook, he turned and announced to no one in particular, "All the waters of the world come together."

Thoreau would have understood. So would the old people in kayaks and canoes.

September/October 1993

The Cruelest Month

I have come to dread the month of April. The officials who rule this community have decreed that any testing to determine the suitability of developable land must be run between the end of March and the beginning of May, when the groundwater levels are generally at their highest. It is not a bad rule, but it has meant that April has become a season of apprehension for those of us in this town who care about the fate of the earth.

One mile from my house there is a field that once served as a horse pasture. Every year in April, usually about the tenth of the month, meadowlarks used to appear in that field and begin staking out their territory. I would hear them singing their plaintive whistle every time I'd walk by, and the song became a sort of signal, one of many in these parts, that spring was upon us, and all was right with the world. But two years ago in April, as I was passing that field, I saw a backhoe parked by the side of the road.

The meadowlarks that turn up in the field each spring are not long-distance migrants. They appear from parts south—just about the time that the forsythia blooms and the grass on the nearby lawns is turning green. The males announce their presence at dawn, and, if you walk by at any time of day and know what to look for, you can see or hear them. They choose a particular rock in the center of the field to broadcast from. Two weeks later, at the beginning of May, you begin to see the females, and for the rest of the season, as the grass grows longer and the spring rolls into summer, you can hear them singing. By late May or June, when the nestlings are hatched in their little covered-over ground nests, the birds quiet down. But, if you watch, you can still see them, sailing past on their kitelike triangular wings.

Later in the week back in that fateful April two years ago, the backhoe moved out into the field and dug a series of trenches. A little later in the day, men with clipboards appeared and stared down into the holes, and that evening, when I went by, the trenches had been refilled. The meadowlarks showed up on schedule a week or so later and set up their territory. But I knew the meaning of the

trenches; they were test holes, and the meadowlarks' fate would be decided by engineers with calculators in sad little offices decorated with calendars of New England past.

Meadowlarks require open grassy fields and pastures for their nest sites. If the grass is too short, as on a golf course or a lawn, they cannot construct their domed, ovenlike nests. If the field grows too old and sprouts long grasses, young trees, or shrubs, they will not nest. And of course, if the field becomes a development, they will not nest. Common logic holds that they will go somewhere else. But current economies have dictated that there is no somewhere else.

In early autumn, after the backhoe appeared in the meadowlarks' pasture, a bulldozer cut a hole in the wall surrounding the meadow and drove what looked like a road directly into the middle of the field and then disappeared.

The field languished in a sort of undeveloped limbo. Then one day the bulldozer reappeared, pushed some more earth around, and a few days later a sign went up announcing a new housing development.

By November more soil had been pushed around. By December foundation holes were dug, and the place that had been a field had evolved into a sort of strip mine, with great spoil piles of soil mounded here and there, bulldozers lurking at the former field edges, a few foundations, and of course mud, a veritable sea of mud.

By January the mud froze and was covered with a blanket of snow. By late March the snow had melted and the mud returned, and on April tenth I heard again the song of meadowlarks in the air.

The meadowlark whistle is a sorrowful little song, repeated over and over. In better times it brings up deep-seated, pleasant associations—greening pastures, flowering crabs, the smell of soil, and a high, windy blue in the air. But last April it sounded what it is: rueful, plaintive, and sad.

North of us in the boreal forest where the majority of passerine birds nest, vast sections of land are clear-cut for pulp to make paper. South of us, in Central and South America, vast sections of forest are cleared for cattle ranches. Here in Massachusetts, in this indeterminate land of mixed hardwoods, suburbs, and fields, there is no such drama; the world declines in bits and pieces.

May/June 1994

A Voice Crying in the Wilderness

The idea of wilderness, of a place apart, is one of the most ancient concepts of human culture. It appears in history shortly after the development of agriculture and by the time of Sumer had evolved into one of the distinguishing features of what we have come to call civilization. By the time of the Old Testament, wilderness was characterized as a barren, desert place, separated from humanity and suited only for wild beasts. Biblical prophets from Moses and Elijah to John the Baptist and Jesus would go apart into the wilderness to reconnect with the wellspring of the universe. In these wild, desert places, among the beasts and empty land, and free from human companionship, they would find solace and spiritual renewal.

The wilderness idea endured through the Greco-Roman era and persisted, even thrived, in Medieval Europe. Monks and mystics would commonly desert the cities and towns to live in the wilds, and whenever they were troubled, or wanted to expiate some sin, heroic Arthurian knights often took to the greenwood, there to spend their days living alone, dressed in green ivy, until some event or epiphany would draw them back into the human community.

Traditionally, here in America, the wilderness was seen as a place that must be conquered—as it seems to be at the beginning of all civilizations. The great deserts and mountains of the American continent were obstacles that had to be overcome in the westward course of empire. It took brawny men and enduring women to cross the Great Plains and Rockies, and the journey consisted in defeating the natural world—wolves, bears, and, most dangerous of all, the races of wild people that inhabited the "wilderness" (a concept, by the way, that was unknown to Native Americans).

Once the continent was tamed, American attitudes changed, and wilderness evolved into a place of solace and renewal, so much so that a whole industry of outfitters, trained to take stressed-out urban and suburban people into the remote spots of the world, developed.

More recently, a realization has come that it is not necessary to go off to the distant places of the world to find peace. For those who care to explore, there are wild places just beyond the backyards of suburbia that offer similar comfort.

At the core of all these wilderness experiences is the long, abiding silence of the land—the existence of a spot, no matter how small, where one can find a quiet place to think. Unfortunately, in the past few decades, all of these places, from the wild reaches of the mountain passes to the woods of suburbia, have been invaded by a plague of noisy recreational machines.

There is something in the American character that seems to require the presence of a powerful machine in order to interact with nature. Now, in the popular mind, in order to get into wilderness, one needs a four-wheel-drive vehicle, a trail bike, a snowmobile, an ORV, ATV, or any one of the many iterations thereof. Even the pursuit of fish, which according to Izaak Walton is one of the most contemplative of human pastimes, has generated in America a vast array of machines, everything from beach buggies to powerful, high-speed bass boats that carry those who are fishing to their chosen sites.

A mere glance at the advertisements in the American media demonstrates the phenomenon in full color—a beautiful wild spot, and, in the midst of all that greenery, a machine. Machines blasting through deep forests and ascending mountains, machines fording streams, machines crossing dunes and deserts—in short, machines overcoming the obstacles presented by nature, even if the obstacles are not a hindrance. One ad even went so far as to describe the machine—a four-wheel-drive vehicle—as "all natural."

These devices, by their very nature, do not encourage the one passive use of wilderness that civilization established—contemplation. Furthermore, because they are often noisy, they discourage contemplation for anyone within their range. They also quite successfully destroy land, uproot native vegetation, and even threaten a wide range of endangered species, everything from manatees to Plymouth gentians to desert tortoises.

Why has it been necessary to develop these powerful machines now, in an age when nature has been unconditionally vanquished, when one cannot go even into the vast reaches of the Arctic and Antarctic without finding signs of human activity, and when grizzly bears, and wolves, and trackless virgin forests are in danger of extinction? It can only be that, while destructive to the natural world, both physically and through the attitudes they encourage, recreational machines are metaphors.

They are the symbols of our power over nature; they evoke atavistic memories of human conquest that date back to the earliest struggles of civilization against the forces of nature.

But in an age when not only wilderness, but the biological structure of the earth itself, is out of balance, we need a new paradigm. Quite clearly, we have won the battle against nature, and now we need to give up our war machines and make a lasting peace with the world.

July/August 1994

Messing About on Beaver Brook

Beaver Brook rises in the swamps of Boxborough, Massachusetts, and flows north-northeast for some ten miles before emptying into Forge Pond in the town of Westford. It's a quiet, sluggish brook, characterized in the main by tea-colored waters, narrow passages through overhanging trees, and, finally, toward the confluence with the pond, by extensive cattail marshes.

In this section, the stream meanders erratically through the marshes, curling along wooded banks, arching out again into the open grasses, curving and recurving back on itself so that, seen from overhead, it takes the form of a snake, slithering northward.

The interior of the marshes is a world apart, a grass-bound passage of slow waters, duckweed, and narrow green hallways, lined, in June and July, with head-high cattails, flowering forget-me-nots, willow herb, wild rice, spatterdock, and arrowhead. In some sections, the vegetation is so thick it blocks out all but a mere channel of blue sky. Ratty and Mole of *The Wind in the Willows* fame would have loved the place.

When I first started exploring Beaver Brook, there was no invasive loosestrife in the cattails, and the waters were deep and cool and periodically opened into round pools where huge snappers lurked. For the first mile, you had to paddle to and fro between high wooded banks, and the air was loud with the songs of marsh wrens and the calls of red-winged blackbirds and swamp sparrows. There were vast deep-throated grumblings from bullfrogs, banjolike twangs from the green frogs, and dark water snakes would periodically disappear into the grassy tangle. There were muskrats and painted turtles, herons and rails. And there were little bands of wood ducks and black ducks that would dash up in terror

whenever you rounded a bend, and then would land again around the next bend, as if out of sight were indeed out of mind.

A mile downstream from the Route 119 bridge, there is a narrow spot where, years past, a farm family in the area maintained a ford. Nowadays, only the heavy granite stones remain. Somewhere along these banks, perhaps near the ford, in the seventeenth century, a Pawtucket Indian named Tom Dublet had a fish weir. Dublet's father was killed by Mohawks at the weir in 1645, and Dublet himself lived somewhere along the brook until his death sometime around 1722. During King Philip's War, in 1675, he acted as a negotiator in the ransom of English captives.

Dublet and the subsequent English families who settled in the immediate area lived with a light touch on the natural environment of Beaver Brook. It wasn't until recently that the marshes began to change dramatically. For one thing, loosestrife, the bane of cattail marshes here in New England, has started to move in. What's worse, a Westford builder constructed a housing development on the high ground on the east side of the brook so that, where once there was a wildwood of deep oaks and hickories, there are now glaring palaces.

Farther downstream, beyond a small timber bridge, the brook grows wild again. Here, in the open expanses of cattail, in informal turtle surveys I used to hold, my children and I once counted more than three hundred painted turtles in the space of a mile. Once we saw a wood turtle, a rare species in the state, on the banks by the bridge, and there were also spotted turtles in the area. I have seen the now-uncommon box turtles in nearby uplands, as well as great blue herons and green herons frequenting this section, and there have been nesting American bitterns, listed as endangered in Massachusetts. Nearby in vernal pools on the floodplain, researchers have recorded the endangered blue-spotted salamander and also the marbled, the most imperiled salamander in the state.

Beaver Brook is changing quickly, but has yet to be destroyed. The western banks are still wild. There are no developments and no nearby houses for nearly two miles; it's all woods, and vernal pools, and overgrown fields where foxes den and owls call by night. But developers have announced plans to reconstruct the timber bridge and begin building on the western banks, and if the permits are granted, to quote ecologist William Beebe in regard to extinction: "...another heaven and another earth must pass before such a one can be again."

November/December 1994

Forgiven Trespasses

On any Saturday morning in May, the birdsong would come rolling in my bedroom from the surrounding hillside long before dawn. I'd be up by sunrise, roll my bicycle out of the garage, and be off for the wider world before the dew was dry on the grass. I was ten, and the backyards were large and brushy and worth finding out about.

There was once money in the town in which I grew up. But by my time all the old families had grown eccentric. Their formal gardens had declined into a weedy patchwork, and frogs and salamanders had taken over their brick-lined swimming pools. Above the town, along the cliffs above the river, the world was even wilder. Here, in the 1920s, well-heeled stockbrokers had constructed larger estates, most of which had been torn down or deserted after the Crash. In the six miles of woods that ran along the cliff, there was rich picking for the unrestrained youths  who ranged in the lower sections. And here, on any given Saturday morning in warm weather, we, the nomadic warriors of our neighborhood, would ascend.

I remember the tract well, a moist mid-Atlantic forest of sweet gum and tulip with the whisperings of gnatcatchers around us, and cerulean warblers, and the lure of ruins. One place in particular held our fancy. The estate was gone, but the pool, with its pergolas and terraces and statuary, was still there. Here we recreated the battles of history. Robin Hood and his band lurked in the surrounding greenwood to sally out and attack King John and his retinue. Here were Indians; here we fought duels in the style of the three musketeers among the moss-strewn statues and the shallow, rain-filled pool. The place, even at this distance in time, looms as a metaphor, a half-remembered country where the true tyrants of our world—parents—held no sway.

There were other sites in town. The old carriage houses, long deserted, had excellent burying grounds in the soils beneath the rotting wood floors. Some had elaborate stairwells, narrow and worth fighting duels to defend. We found the bodies of rats and possums and raccoons in these old barns, and we sent the resident pigeons aloft in wild flurries. One building even had a barn owl, I was told, but this we avoided inasmuch as it was carefully guarded by someone's eccentric uncle.

The town had streams and stone bridges over roadways into which large drainage pipes emptied. We had read or seen the movie *Les Misérables*, with its famous sewer scenes, and these too we replayed periodically. We tunneled down grates, through narrow spots, and into larger conduits that fed to the bridges and the brooks. Once beneath one of these bridges, a companion was attacked by a vicious muskrat who lunged at his throat, teeth bared—so he claimed—but only managed to get a bite out of his thumb.

It was here, in this landscape, that we learned the art of survival. It was here that I came to understand territory. Children, evil children from other parts of town, would sometimes sally forth and invade our grounds, and so we recapitulated history and defended our land with sticks and showers of stones from one of the old barns where we maintained our Fortress America against the Nazis, the king's militia, marauding knights, pirates, renegade cowboys, bands of thirties-style gangsters, and those myriad imaginary enemies of all forms who would assault our ground.

We found nests, we caught frogs and put them into our mouths on a dare, we collected salamanders and put them in fish tanks to watch them grow, we pulled clumps of onion grass from the moist earth and showered one another, we scaled the peaked roofs of a large nearby church. We brought home to nurse poor pigeons and English sparrows, along with baby rabbits, moles, and mice the cats carried in. Oscar the crow, who my brother rescued and who lived with us for years, always fixed me with his glinty eye if I ever came near him when my brother was not around.

There were no boy scouts in this tribe. There were no after-school programs. Saturday-morning television held no attraction, and personal computers, to my eternal gratitude, had yet to be invented. We were bounded only by the wilderness of our own imaginations. But, there are times when, staring at the child-empty fields and woods around the town in which I now live, I wonder in what fields the children of this lost generation of wanderers play.

May/June 1997

The River Road

Someday in the early summer, I'm going to dress in a Panama hat, white ducks, and saddle shoes, borrow my brother's 1947 Chevrolet, and drive to Vermont with my wife. She'll wear a cotton shirtwaist dress, white sneakers, and a brimmed straw hat with a blue ribbon. We'll start early, drive on back roads to Brattleboro, then turn north on Route 5 and watch the Connecticut River landscape roll by.

For the next two days, driving slowly, we'll keep the river on our right, and, whenever we come to a likely field at midday, we'll take our straw picnic basket and go down by the shore, eat cold chicken, and lean on our elbows in the afternoon, watching the old river run by and the play of the wind in the trees on the right bank.

Nowadays, the drive from southern Connecticut to the northeast kingdom of Vermont can be accomplished in three to four hours, if you push the speed limit and the traffic is light. But in my time, when my family and I would undertake this same journey, it took three days. Five of us. My father in his white ducks and saddle shoes, my mother in a shirtwaist dress and a straw hat, and the three of us in back, counting cupolas and the round barns of Vermont, waving our arms out the windows in the wind, and asking if we were there yet when we still had two days worth of driving to do.

My father worked as the "doctor" in a boys' camp just north of East Charleston, Vermont (he wasn't a real doctor, so I don't know how or why he got the job). Each summer in June, we would roll up the rugs, cover the furniture with sheets, catch the dog, and drive along the river to Vermont.

We would come up the Merritt Parkway (counting bridges all the way; there were fifty-six as I recall), and as soon as we could, we'd cut over to the Connecticut River and drive up the left bank, staying in big white hotels and listening to the whistle of the night trains switching at White River Junction. The journey marks the best times in my memory—the end of school, the beginning of a long summer, the smell of fresh-cut hay, the smell of the first spruces of the

north, the smell of river water, and the view of that rolling Connecticut River landscape, where the sky drops down to the hay field, and the fields drop down to the river, and the river runs down to the sea.

A few years ago, starting this time at Brattleboro, I began annually recreating this sentimental journey. The thing that first struck me is that it can still be done. You can still spot the vernacular landscape of the river road of the 1940s and early 1950s—the rusting Jenny gas signs, the old decaying round barns with hay spilling out of their lofts, the cow yards, the cupolas, the pastures and fields. And always, sometimes out of sight, sometimes dominating the view, the Connecticut, the Great River, as it used to be called by the Indians, the winding river, the silver light river, the gray light river, blue light river, snaking through the hay fields, curving east, curving west, now wide and slow, now running hard through highlands, collecting tributaries all along the way, and never ceasing in its downslope southbound quest for the mother sea.

July/August 1998

A Paradise of Frogs

Years ago I saw a photograph of Mark Twain in his summer whites, standing beside a frog pond with a cane pole fishing rod in his hands. It was his custom, I was told, to tie strips of meat to the end of a line and feed his bullfrogs for entertainment on summer afternoons. The image haunted me for years.

The place where I now live was once a paradise of frogs. There was a fallen barn on the property and an old uncut lawn in back of the house with a few apple trees, backed by deep woods, complete with vernal pools. The yard, early on, was characterized mainly by amphibians. Wherever I walked, it seemed that something cold-blooded was hopping out of the way, either a toad, a wood frog, or sometimes a green frog. I used to keep the pasture grasses down with a scythe, and, nearly every other swing, sleek-bodied pickerel frogs would execute fantastic crisscrossing leaps to escape. I once found a gray treefrog in a hole in one of the old apple trees while I was out scything, and, sometimes, after long rainy spells in spring, we would find frogs inside the very house—wood frogs in the cellar, spring peepers in the kitchen, and, once, a gray treefrog on the dining room window.

Slowly, in the perhaps mistaken course of gentrification of these grounds, I began mowing the lawn and digging in flower beds and cleaning up the fallen barn and the assorted detritus that had collected there ever since the old farmer who once owned this place went to his reward. The constant annual scything of the grasses under the apple trees finally evicted the poison ivy and the multiflora rose and the blackberry. But the pickerel frogs also departed. Toads no longer hopped out of the way on hot summer nights when you crossed a stone terrace in the back of the house, and I rarely saw any frogs on my lawn. What's worse, development began creeping into the former fields and woods around the house, and, sadly, year by year, the spring peeper chorus diminished, and I heard less and less of the beautiful birdlike trilling of the gray treefrogs.

Part of this may have been a sign of the general worldwide decline in frog populations, but I considered that, at least around my property, it was probably all my own handiwork and that my cleaning up projects had forced them out. As a result, some years ago, I started to do something to try to bring them back.

My first act was to dig a frog pond under the apple trees. This was just a shallow, scooped-out area that I lined with concrete. I dug the pond in March, let the concrete set, and then filled it on a rainy day in early April. The next morning I looked out from the back porch and saw a toad sitting on a rock I had placed in a shallow end. Unfortunately, within a week the frog pond began to drain itself. I filled it again, and it leaked out once more. I bought sealer and painted the bottom to no avail, and in the end I had to go out and buy one of those little pre-made fishponds. To disguise its inherent ugliness, I gave this liner a skim coat of cement and then filled it. A week later, no fewer than three green frogs moved in.

Inspired by this, I dug out another small pond farther from the house and put in another pre-made fishpond someone had given me. Within a few days, more green frogs took up residence, and, at the end of the summer, a fine pickerel frog settled there, along with a fat bullfrog.

I had no illusions that a single backyard frog pond, or for that matter

10,000 backyard frog ponds spread out across the suburbs of America, would do anything to halt habitat destruction or the mysterious worldwide decline of frogs. The fact is, I like frogs. I like to have them around. My pond projects were not that much different from maintaining a backyard bird feeder.

To further encourage my frogs, I stopped mowing grass with a lawn mower and resumed scything. With the poison ivy evicted from the grounds under the apple trees, I allowed the grasses to grow all season, save for one or two cuts to keep the woody plants out. I let weeds take over former garden patches and allowed brush to grow along the back walls. I built several little toolsheds that were intended not necessarily for tools but to serve as hiding places for mice and snakes, and eves for nesting birds, and a sanctuary for toads to hide underneath in the heat of the day. And, finally, although it's not yet complete, I began digging out a larger, deeper frog pond just beyond the apple trees.

My hope is that someday I will attract a permanent bullfrog population. And then in summer, I shall dress in a white suit, tie meat strips to a fishing line, and spend the rest of my days feeding frogs.

May/June 1999

An Amphibian Bill of Rights

Bill #24D 630: An Act to Prohibit Driving on Suburban and Rural Roads on Rainy Nights Between March and October.

It was not, as W.C. Fields might have said, a night fit for man or beast. It had been sheeting down with rain since dawn, and everywhere in the woods little silvered raindrops were hanging from the swelling buds in the half-light. By nightfall, some of the brooks had risen and there was a great deal of talk of local flooding. Not a night you would want to be on the roads, nor in the woods, nor tramping around in shallow ponds, nor viewing cherry blossoms. But it was a very good night for salamanders and frogs.

I took my daughter up to the Robinson's Swamp to see if the salamanders that normally breed there had arrived. We could hear the spring peepers calling long before we got there, and once we got onto Robinson Road it took us a long time to get up to the swamp because every ten yards I'd see another one of those white twigs in the headlights and have to stop the car. I knew from experience that these "white twigs" were in fact salamanders, and so I had to pull over, stop the car, put on the blinkers, get out, and risk my life issuing the poor things from one side of the road to the next before some other driver winged by and squashed them. And then fifty yards farther along, there would be another one. And in between, I'd see those little white pebbles in the headlights that turned out to be spring peepers, or wood frogs, and have to stop again and wait while they made up their minds to hop on.

And this was only the beginning.

We had had a few nights like this earlier, three to be exact, but this was what those who follow this sort of thing term "the big night." The storm was engulfing the entire region, and anywhere outside of a major city, and in some cases perhaps even within a major city, there would be frogs and salamanders in the road. And this was, as I say, only the beginning.

To my knowledge, no one has ever been able to calculate just how many frogs and salamanders emerge from their winter hibernation in a given region on a given night like this and move through woodlands and fields, meadows, people's backyards, and even parking lots—crossing, wherever necessary, the back roads of suburbia and what used to be termed the countryside (whatever that means in this age of decentralized settlements when every other new house seems to back onto a ten-thousand-year-old wetland where frogs and salamanders mate and lay their eggs).

Furthermore, no one to my knowledge has ever been able to determine just how many of those migratory amphibians are killed on a rainy night in spring when they are on the move.

I do know this. I know that I have been out on certain roads, on certain warm rainy nights in late spring when the green frogs are on the move, and I have stepped out of the car and I have been able to smell—not necessarily see, mind you, but, actually, smell—the odor of dead frogs. It's a distinct scent, not even a bad odor, more of a wet, muddy, froggy sort of smell.

I know of a woman who annually stands by a road near her house with a flashlight and flags down cars when "her" frogs are moving from their breeding pools to a nearby lake. One night she counted 278 frogs on the move. Even with her vigilance, 47 of them died under the wheels of impatient drivers that night. Another friend has stopped walking the road in front of her house on mornings following heavy rains. The hundreds of "smushed frogs," as she phrases it, are too much to bear.

For years I used to think that when I get old and crazy, I will become one of those persistent devils who legislators see in the halls of the State House, a disheveled, harmless old fellow, with a bizarre mission and a leather briefcase spilling over with documents containing frog and salamander mortality statistics as well as

signed petitions proposing a bill that would do something, finally, to halt the slaughter of frogs and salamanders on roads. Such a bill, I am informed, would be laughed out of the halls of the legislature. But who cares? I'm serious about it. There are too many roads, and too few frogs, and I don't care what anyone says about "progress" and the need for access, and traffic volumes, and curb cuts, and the fact that people must have homes, and that roads have to be built to get to said homes, and that in order to do that local wetlands where frogs and salamanders breed have to be filled.

If people want to get home on rainy nights, let them walk from train stations on footpaths. But that too, at least from the point of view of a human being, would seem absurd.

Frogs might not see it that way, though.

March/April 2001

The Ultimate Alien

There are indications that one of the most nefarious forest pests ever to arrive in North America may have attempted to establish itself on the continent as many as a thousand years ago. There is also evidence of later contact, especially along the Northeastern coasts. But it was not until some five hundred years ago that permanent colonies took root. The species appeared first on islands in the Caribbean, moved west to Florida, then to the interior of Mexico, and then began spreading itself northward. Within a hundred years, it made substantial inroads into North America, and, by the mid-seventeenth century, it had set up permanent colonies.

Not unlike leafcutter ants, termites, beavers, and a few others, this species tended to alter the habitats in those areas where it established its colonies. Like its fellow mammal, the beaver, its normal feeding habits required that it cut down trees. Unlike beavers, however, this species also tended to alter the architecture of the native soils. It not only felled the local trees but rooted in the soils to encourage the growth of plants upon which it would feed, many that it had imported from its native Europe.

The actual makeup of the native American forests before the arrival of the pest is much debated. There are some theories that suggest that the great Atlantic forest consisted of immense towering trees that so shaded the forest floor that wide vistas of parklike lands stretched beneath them. Newer thinking holds that these mixed forests consisted of smaller younger trees and a thick understory of brush—the theory being that, except in certain sheltered areas, the forests were constantly subjected to pruning by insects, fires, and storms. In either case, although there were wide glades and openings and extensive beaver meadows along streams in some areas, it is generally agreed that these mid-Atlantic forests stretched from the east coast to the Mississippi. The old homily was that a squirrel could cross from the coast to the Plains without ever touching ground.

But it was all doomed.

The generally accepted figure is that by the midnineteenth century, because of

its feeding patterns and because the new-coming species used wood to construct its dens and lodges and even developed the habit of intentionally burning the wood, the great Atlantic forests were reduced to a mere 15 percent of their original size. The mammalian and avian species that lived in these forests before the sixteenth century were considered some of the most diverse on earth. But, as the invader moved west, these declined dramatically. As early as 1700 in some sections of the East, bears, moose, wolves, whitetail deer, cougars, and turkeys had been killed off, forcing the new-coming predator to range farther west in its hunting forays.

Like many of the most destructive aliens, the invaders were omnivorous. The general pattern was that the more predatory individuals would move into the forests to those frontiers as yet unspoiled and would be followed by the less vicious but more destructive herbivores. This pattern progressed over a period of three centuries, eliminating some of the most common species of the forest east of the Mississippi: the wood bison, wapiti, moose, beaver, mountain lion, bear, wolf, bobcat, lynx, and a number of smaller animals such as the fisher. Some of these native species were driven to extinction as a result of the forest decline and the predation of newcomers. Of these, the most dramatic was the case of the passenger pigeon whose numbers were once so great as to darken the skies for days during their annual migrations.

The earth is nothing if not resilient, however; and a new forest has returned to much of the cleared land. This new forest may be threatened yet again by other forces, but at least the alien species that first leveled the trees has now adapted—one hopes—to its new environment and comprehends that such a disaster should not come again.

May/June 2001

The Go-Between

I once spent some time in the Azores, back in the days when so-called "primitive" whaling from open boats was still legal. One afternoon from the deck of one of the little inter-island steamers, I happened to see a whale hunt in progress. A small motor vessel was in the process of towing a string of the light Yankee whaleboats out toward a pod of spouting sperm whales. As the fleet approached the pod, the powerboat dropped its string of whale hunters and motored off some distance, and the little open boats set sail and began rowing and tacking toward the gamboling whales.

A local fellow I knew onboard, whose full name translated to something like "Manny the Man," pointed the hunt out to me, and I spent an hour or two watching the action with him through my binoculars. Manny had once been a whaler himself, and, as we watched, he described the details of the process to me. The crew, he said, was made up of sixteen- or seventeen-year-old island boys who, when the whales were spotted from a watchtower on the island of Fayal, would be summoned to the harbor by a siren. They'd put out to sea, towed by the powerboat, and then, because the Azoreans believe that the whales were frightened by the sound of the engines, would sail and row after their prey. In typical Yankee style, they would row up to striking distance of a surfaced whale, harpoon it, allow the whale to run out the line, and then begin the long, arduous work of hauling in the "fixed" whale. The carcass would then be towed back to a shoreside whale station where it would be flensed and tried out for its oil.

From where I stood on the foredeck that afternoon, it looked like the boys weren't having much luck that day. They'd sail after the spouting whales, which would sound and then reappear in another quarter-mile, sometimes half-mile astern of the little group of whaleboats. The crew would turn and sail off in the other direction, trying to catch up with them. All afternoon the little troop of whalers tacked back and forth in the waters off Fayal in this manner, apparently without success.

Truth be told, I was rooting for the whales. These were the first sperm whales

I had ever seen, and these vast marine mammals were almost a part of my soul. I grew up in a family that considered Melville's *Moby Dick* some manner of sacred text, and the art of hunting whales from small fragile craft to be the consummation of seafaring. Unfortunately, however, as I later learned from Manny, the boys killed eleven sperm whales that afternoon.

Part of my attraction to the sperm whale is the downright inscrutability of this animal. The ur-whale, *Moby Dick*, was a sperm whale, and in my childhood the mystique of this great creature was made all the more real by a haunting display in the halls of the American

Museum of Natural History in New York. A sperm whale in the exhibition was locked in shadowed battle with that other mysterious denizen of the deep, the giant squid, or kraken.

Sperm whales are rarely, if ever, seen on the ever-popular whale watches. They range the blue waters of the world and prefer the great depths such as the chasms off the Mid-Atlantic Ridge. They can dive to depths of more than half a mile and stay submerged for over an hour, and they can swim at a speed of twelve knots, easily outpacing rowed whaleboats. Their favorite food is the deepwater species of medium-sized squid, but they will also eat fish and octopus and normally consume a ton of food a day. They are, in effect, animals of two worlds: they know the murky unlit mysteries of the deep; but they're also air-breathing mammals that know the look of the open sea and the sky. They are toothed with great five- to eight-inch teeth that, as we know from *Moby Dick*, are capable of snapping off a sea captain's leg or crushing a whaleboat. Manny the Man gave me two of these menacing teeth as a parting gift when I left Fayal, not realizing that under the Marine Mammal Protection Act I could not legally bring them into the United States.

Later that evening the steamer put into Horta on Fayal, and, after sipping a fortifying drink at the then-popular Cafe de Sport, a favorite watering hole of yachtsmen, I wandered over to the whale factory. There, on the skids, lay one of the whales from the afternoon hunt, a tragic still behemoth grounded out on the wet cobbles, its gray black thick skin gleaming in the light rain.

Seeing this vast creature dragged from its natural environment and knowing what I knew about the world of whales, the romance of traditional whaling, or what was left of it, was over.

July/August 2002

The Breakup

The second winter that I lived in the stone cottage above the brook the snows began in mid-November. There was a blizzard on December 8 and, following that, week after week of periodic snowfall, some of it heavy, some simply a steady dusting that drifted down between the surrounding pines. Streams in the valleys iced up early that year; the lake froze solid by mid-December, and there were a few snowy nights there when we might have believed that the world beyond that little valley had come to an end and we were alone with the dog and a good supply of firewood.

January passed. February became old; some days we skied down to the hollow where Hurricane Brook cut through the ravine and cleared the snow from the deeper pools and lay facedown on the ice. Beneath, we could hear the growl and rumble of running water, and one day there, later in the month, I spotted an oblong open hole in the ice. I sank to my knees and stared. There below, I could see a swirling rush of black water.

Finally, imperceptibly at first, the snows began to melt. There was a smell of something in the air, something moist. The little icicles appeared at the ends of the twigs of the sugar maples that lined the road to the cottage. The days slowly warmed, the spring songs of the titmice and the chickadees filled the woods, and one afternoon, down by the swamp below the cottage, I saw the little green noses of skunk cabbage and the curled cigars of false hellebore poking up through the sphagnum and the mud.

In early March there was a hard rain that turned to ice as the evening wore on, and late that night there was a precipitous drop in the temperature and a hard freeze. Early in the morning, I dreamed of a burnished crystal palace. The dream, in fact, was real. The surrounding forest was gleaming in celestial light, every twig, every branch and bud, was glistering in the sun. Then the day warmed, and all morning we could hear the clatter of falling ice.

In effect this event marked the end.

One night about this time I was awakened by a profound, incessant roaring. At first, in the confusion of half-drugged winter sleep, I thought some vast freight train was passing in the valley below. But this little cottage was set in the middle of 40,000 acres of wildland, and there were no rail lines within fifty miles. There were hardly any roads, in fact; but the roaring sounded like some distant, heavily traveled superhighway cutting through the wilderness. I thought perhaps a high wind had come up and was raging through the bare limbs; I had heard such  sounds at the beginning of winter, with the onset of storms. But I looked out the window and the entire world was still. I got dressed and went outside.

It was a peaceful, warm night with a quarter-moon descending beyond the basketwork of the winter woods. Outside the noise was even louder; it thundered above the trees like a squadron of propeller-driven warplanes, a disembodied sound that rode through the upper air. I couldn't place the origin. I heard the sound to the north, where Hurricane Brook cut throughout the ravine. I could hear it coming up from the south, above the swamp and the lake and the valleys west of the lake. I heard it in the sky; it seemed to emerge from the very earth. It permeated even the granite walls of the cottage. And then finally I figured out what it was.

This region was characterized by high hills and deep valleys, a large lake, and many running streams. On this singular night, after weeks of slow warming and periodic rains, all the streams of all the valleys had, as a body, freed themselves from the chain of ice that had bound them winter long. Free at last, they came charging through their streambeds, crashing ever downward to larger streams and thence to small rivers, and then onto the mother of all rivers in these parts, the Connecticut, and then, finally, to the sea.

And after that night, it was spring. The wood frogs began croaking in the hollows. The spring peepers called, the salamanders emerged from their deep burrows and marched through the woods, arbutus bloomed, the red-wings came back, and for the first time since early November you could smell earth, and the forest and redolent odor of that quintessential elixir of all life—water.

Spring 2003

Night of the Falling Stars

Long ago, when we lived successfully disguised to ourselves as sailors, my oldest brother and I were hired to deliver a schooner from Maine to Stonington, Connecticut. In point of fact, we were probably too young to be trusted with such work; and since we had no specific date for the actual delivery, rather than make a straight run of the affair, we spent the whole month of August sailing slowly along the coast, poking into little anchorages along the way, stopping often to explore. Toward the middle of the month, having had our fill of salty ports crowded with New York yachts, we came into a small, unpopulated, unhoused cove on one of the Elizabeth Islands and dropped anchor.

That evening we lounged on the afterdeck and watched the night slither in across the moors and low hills to our west. The wind dropped after dark, and the waters of the cove merely riffled against the hull. We could hear frogs and the occasional croak of a night-heron, and then, one by one, from all across the island, whip-poor-wills began to call. It was hot, a sultry night, with the tribes of stars floating overhead and our little vessel suspended between the unfathomable depths of black waters below and black skies above.

By this time on our cruise, having been alone for so long, and living as we were under the open skies, my brother began to imagine that we had descended from some lost race of lean bronzed gods, capable of anything. From time to time, in order to prove this fact to visiting sailorettes, my brother had developed the habit of ascending the mainstays, standing on the crosstrees, and then diving headlong from the topmast of the schooner, barely clearing the gunnels in the process. Now, in the close stillness and the flickering heat lightning from the distant shores, he announced that he was going for a swim and began clambering up the mainstay.

I watched as his dark monkeylike form shimmied higher and higher. Just before he reached the crosstrees, a shooting star arched out of the black sky over his head and burnt itself out. He gained his foothold and stood upright, steadying himself with one hand on the topmast. Then he raised his arms above his head and

balanced momentarily. Two more stars flared out and disappeared. He crouched slightly, raised himself up, and then like a gannet, he speared outward and downward.

It was a good dive, one of his best. He seemed to fall in slow-motion, and as his outstretched figure moved across the sky and the black shores, a host of shooting stars, one after the other, dashed out above him. He sailed forward, unbounded, as if he had somehow slipped the chains of gravity, and for a moment it seemed to me that all time was contained between the waters and the stars. He had in fact converted himself into some form of celestial being, one of his lean gods. All around him, as he dove, he trailed stars in a veritable explosion of light. The stars descended with him toward the black depths of the cove, and, when he struck, they followed him into the depths in a great trailing curtain of light, denser now and more brilliant.

It was only when I saw his submerged figure halt, turn, and begin rising again, splaying stars outward with every stroke, that I realized he was spilling off phosphorescent plankton and not celestial bodies.

Later, much later, and in more boring adult hours, I learned that we had lain in that dark harbor at the height of one of the best Perseid meteor showers in decades. Likewise, the stars of the lower depths were caused by bioluminescence resulting from the excitation of cells of tiny dinoflagellates that move within the sun-warmed waters of New England each year in late summer.

But all that, in the end, is mere science, and in those brighter years he and I lived outside of the confines of science and reality—or so we believed.

Summer 2003

The Flight of the Wren

On any given morning between May 5 and May 10, I can step out in the garden and hear, for the first time in a year, the incessant, even frenetic, trilling of the house wren. They come in with the south wind, usually on a clear sunny morning, and go out, with far less flourish, on the northwest wind five months later.

The male is the first to arrive, and he goes around "his" land (which according to twenty-first-century legal documents is actually "my" land) stating his ownership in no uncertain terms. He's been here before, and he knows his way around.

The female arrives a few days later. And after a certain amount of ritual, and restatements of territorial boundaries—none of which I can follow—she will begin work on a nest in a palatial birdhouse I have set up in back of the garden. The two of them spend the spring and summer there. Flitting around, getting angry, and hunting through the shrubbery for spiders and caterpillars.

Bird aficionados are not supposed to like wrens. They're noisy little devils, for one thing, and they have some very nasty habits. Once they've crammed their bulky stick nests into whatever convenient crevice they can find, they range around their property pecking the eggs of other nesting birds, almost out of spite, it would seem. Furthermore, they are not—how shall I say—the most beautiful bird in the backyard. They are patterned with a few dark stripes against a dull wood-colored brown background, their belly is whitish, and they have a mean little decurved bill that looks like it was designed for surgical purposes. Nor are they loyal mates. Once they have set up housekeeping, and the female is incubating the eggs, the male patrols his territory seeking other females. Given all  this, they have not endeared themselves to those who seek wholesome metaphors from the world of birds—even their semi-musical trilling becomes tedious when you hear it every minute or so throughout the daylight hours.

In spite of all this, I am partial to wrens. I like their spunk. I like their cocky little tails and beady eyes, and the way they get mad at anything in their path and begin whispering and chattering at cats and dogs and even people.

But mostly what I like about wrens is their predestined willingness to undertake marathon flights from the cold gardens of New England and Canada, south to Florida, and even beyond into Central and South America. It seems somehow unfathomable that these tiny packages can summon the energy to fly all the way down a continent and back up in the course of a year, select mates, and then go about the business of raising children, only to turn around and go back south again in autumn.

Sometime in the summer, I don't know when exactly since they slip out quietly, the wrens leave my garden. They fade from the sunny borders and move back into the shady woods, where they spend the late summer and early autumn feeding low to the ground, no longer singing and assuming a certain hardworking, businesslike effect. Perhaps they need to lay low in this manner. They have a long trip ahead of them.

Although a few individuals may hang around the northern woods until November, most house wrens begin their mass exodus in September. Like many land birds, they move south in fits and starts; and, like many migrants, they run into hardships all along the way. Storms carry them far out to sea. Headwinds batter them, cats eat them, and, along with a growing number of birds nowadays, wrens crash into things at night. Fifty years ago these obstacles were radio towers, water towers, and the skyscrapers of cities. Now the birds have to contend with the proliferation of cell phone towers as well.

Somehow, through all this, through pure atavistic drive and that unstoppable wren energy, they make it.

Wrens are not long-distance migrants in the manner of swifts and nighthawks, or even warblers and hummingbirds. They generally only go as far south as Florida. But it is that lack of limelight, that commonplace, dogged manner that I like about them. They're energetic little sparks of life in a hard rock world. I daresay they will never become extinct.

Fall 2003

El Lobo

Once I inherited a Jack Russell terrier, who for some reason promptly chose me as his boon companion in his otherwise circumscribed life. If I went for a walk to the hemlock grove behind my house, he would join me, ranging out ahead of me in ever-widening gyres, and poking his black nose into every hole, log hollow, rock crevice, tree crevice, leaf pile, brush pile, puddle, and pit he could find. In the garden he was also there, standing by my side, ever at alert, his head cocked, watching my work intently. And if ever I was on my knees with my hands deep in the good earth—about at his level in other words—I would hear his snuffling and glance over. There he'd be, cheek by jowl, eyes fixed on the ground, ears perked forward, ready for some action. In time I taught him to dig out weeds, and even trained him to dig holes for tulip planting.

His other work with us was to protect the property from intruders, which to his dogly mind were legion. There were known to be bears, wolves, foxes, wild ungulates, and all manner of unidentified species lurking in the forest beyond the garden wall. We ourselves could not always see these beasts, and we often wondered why, on some otherwise quiet afternoon, the dog would charge out from the porch and race along the top of the stone wall, barking insanely as if holding at bay a primordial herd of invading mammoths or a rangy pack of dire wolves from the time when this little patch of earth was all forest and swamp.

One afternoon, while I was working in the garden, I heard my companion barking furiously in the woods beyond the back wall. Nothing out of the ordinary really, except that he would return periodically to my side, circle my ankles, and charge out again into the alien forest to resume his barking, which I noticed had a slightly different, more frenetic (if that's possible) timbre to it. It occurred to me that he had treed something, and, after a while, I went out to see what it was. It turned out he was holding at bay the largest, wildest coyote I have ever seen.

Most of the coyotes that periodically cross this property are skittish things that tentatively flit over the walls to feed on compost. If they see you, or hear you, or even think they see you, they fade into the forest. But this animal was a fearless Goliath, and he was standing his ground—a great, gray and brown, furred, wolflike thing with a wide head, his forelegs propped on a low rock, staring back at this little canine poseur who circled at a safe distance, yapping. I realized, if he so chose, he could step down and with one snap do away with my loyal companion. So I stepped forward and waved my arms.

Rather than dash away, the coyote merely sauntered off indifferently, took a stand on another boulder, and turned to look back. The dog charged after it, circling and barking with even more ferocity, having presumed, I suppose, that he believed he had got the better of this devil dog. I called him off with a whistle and clapped my hands to scare away the intruder and returned to the garden, the dog at my heels.

We saw this coyote on several occasions after this event. We would sometimes spot him standing on a wide stone wall that runs along the west side of the property, the morning sun gleaming off his gray-gold fur. Another time we saw him saunter across the yard, glancing over at the house periodically, straight-legged and spoiling for a fight. He became a commonality. He even earned a name: El Lobo. We actually came to appreciate him for his wildness.

It was about this same time that I learned that his wolflike appearance was no accident. New genetic studies on the origins of the eastern coyote seemed to indicate that, genetically, they were far closer to the original New England wolf, a subspecies of the red wolf, than they were to the simpering little coyotes of the West. He and his type had returned to their native forest habitat along with the bears, fishers, bobcats, whitetail deer, and other denizens of the primordial forest that grew back in New England after the region lost most of its farmland.

Twice over the following year, the Jack Russell stood El Lobo off again. Once at the stone wall next to the garden and once when, for no apparent reason, the coyote appeared in the middle of the vegetable garden among the tomato plants and the chard, glaring back at the house. On both these occasions, alerted by the barking of my assistant, I was the one who ultimately drove El Lobo away.

Later that winter, however, there was a third standoff.

We had a big, disorganized group of people at Christmas Eve dinner that year. Late in the evening, one of the guests went out on the porch and found the Jack Russell by the back door, his head hanging low, in apparent defeat. He walked

in, slowly, an almost unheard of gait for him, and we noticed that he had a bloodied shoulder and that his unbounded, unstoppable energy seemed to have drained out of him. I gathered him up and found deep bite wounds all around his shoulders. Wasting no time, we had him bundled and raced him off to a nearby animal emergency center, which, having determined that he had been badly mauled, sent us off to the Tufts University School of Veterinary Medicine in North Grafton.

This begat an ironic night drive through the darkened landscape of rural New England, when all the world was stuffed and sleeping off the full dinners of Christmas Eve. The dog was admitted, and the vet, a refined gentleman from one of the southern states, said that he was not sure the dog would survive the night, but they would do what they could.

We drove home and waited for the dreaded call. When it came, around seven, we were informed that he was still alive.

He lived through the second night. He rallied, lived through the third night, and was released a week later, much battered, barely able to walk, but still counting himself among the living. At his exit interview from the hospital, the vet explained that he had been picked up and shaken by a large animal, probably a coyote, but that he must have put up a very good fight.

"I imagine," he said in his lazy drawl, "that he must have got in a few good bites."

Maybe he did. After that night, the woods were still. The great horned owls began calling in the hemlock grove in late January. In February the snows began melting back slowly, and by March the wood frogs began calling from the nearby vernal pool.

But after that terrible Christmas Eve we never did see El Lobo again.

Spring 2004

Chasing the Chat

The yellow-breasted chat is described in various ornithological tomes and field guides as an infrequent and irregular summer visitor in Massachusetts. It is a catbird-sized creature with a yellow breast and a mockingbirdlike song and, as far as habitat is concerned, it favors catbrier thickets and patches of dense undergrowth. Although it is rarely actually seen in Massachusetts, it nests from the Cape and the southern part of the state all the way north to the Berkshires, and sometimes even spends the winter here.

But where exactly does one find this elusive chat and how would one go about actually seeing it?

On an otherwise normal day back in 1995, I was drifting down the Nissitissit River in southern New Hampshire, not thinking of anything very much at all save the languorous beauties of a June day and the pleasures of the coming summer, when I heard a sad little warbling and mewing emanating from a brushy meadow on the left bank. I thought it was a mockingbird at first and then remembered a line from one of the many bird identification books describing the song of the furtive chat. I sat up abruptly and looked over my shoulder as the bird warbled on and the river carried me off.

Not to be outfoxed by mere downstream currents, I back paddled and steered the boat toward the shore, intending to land and find the singer. By that point the river had narrowed, the current increased, and before I could make the turn the bow was swept downstream again. No matter; I paddled hard on the port side to reach quieter water on the right bank to paddle upstream and try again. But in midriver the current increased once more and carried me toward a huge rock, festooned with deadly tree snags. More hard paddling, the canoe listing and almost shipping water, whereupon a small, energetic dog I had with me either fell overboard in his excitement or decided it was time for a swim and began a furious dog-paddle for the right bank, all the while sweeping downstream. I turned the boat again, skirted the rock with its armor of deadly snags, made the shore on the right bank, retrieved the dog, and then carried on downstream.

But no chat.

That was in June. In July that same year, I was on the north shore of Martha's Vineyard walking along on the Rock Bight Trail, not thinking of chats, or much else for that matter. At one point the trail I was following broke out from the oak scrub and passed though an open glade of blueberry, thickets of catbrier, and low brush. There it was again, the sweet low chattering and whistling.

I squinted into the thicket and moved toward the sound. Something fluttered in the thickets, and I stepped deeper into the greenwood tangle and waited. Silence. Only the sound of the field crickets and the dull thud of the waves down on the beach. The bird began to chatter again and I pursued more vigorously—much scratched by catbrier, poison ivy all around me, disease-bearing ticks abounding. Then I saw a shadowy form spirit off and drop down into a hollow well beyond a high impenetrable wall of catbrier.

No chat.

All this occurred at the end of a much longer quest. Earlier, maybe even ten years earlier, in Old Lyme, Connecticut, not far from the riverbank home of the famous Roger Tory Peterson himself, my brother and I were walking toward the shore through an apparently deserted old field. At one point, I saw a yellowish bird rise up out of the brush, its legs suspended, and then drop down into the thickets again. Here I was in the very heartland of Lyme disease, barelegged and hot, ticks, mosquitoes, poison ivy, and catbrier everywhere. Undeterred, I gave chase; yet to no avail the bird had disappeared.

As I threaded my way back toward my brother, there came a hideous roaring and I saw a sweating baboonlike man with a red face and red bandana headband just emerging from a battered jeep, already cursing my brother mightily and informing him in no uncertain terms that this was private property and that my brother and his type (not sure what his type was exactly) should get the hell out and stay off his private land or he would hold us until the police arrived. My thought was to hide in the thickets and let my brother take the fall. But the enraged landowner spotted me and started shouting again, pointing at me aggressively. I tried to assuage him with a stuttering nerdy explanation of my plight, that is to say, my lifelong desire to observe the elusive and rare bird called the yellow-breasted chat—a *rara avis* indeed, otherwise known, in the Linnaean system of nomenclature, as *Icteria virens*. This managed to disarm him briefly, and we were permitted to exit his property without a police escort.

But still no chat.

And so it went, year after year. A dog attack in Westport. Lost in the thickets of Chatham. A strange encounter with another offended landowner who actually took an interest in my quest and insisted on showing me all the improvements he was making to his newly acquired holdings (which in the eyes of an environmentalist were no improvements at all). And on one occasion, as I was emerging from reservoir land in southeastern Connecticut, a police interrogation. Why was I there on land that was clearly marked off-limits? And my car illegally parked to boot? I explained that I was taking part in a national survey of a certain species of nesting bird known as the yellow-breasted chat. (Not exactly true, but mostly true—this was my own private survey and I had so far ranged from southern New Hampshire to Florida in my search.) This, I was informed, did not excuse me from walking on private holdings without written permission. Once again I was released with a mere warning.

And then finally, again, on the Nissitissit, one year ago. The same slow drift, the same meadow, the same warbling song, and, just before the current caught me, a yellow bird rose out of the brush, flitted off in a lilting flight, legs dangling in the style of chats, and dropped down again just before the river bore me away.

But was it in fact a chat? Such fleeting confirmation, so brief a showing for such an elusive a bird. Inadmissible evidence in any court of law.

Summer 2005

Place and Remembrance

The great American naturalist Edwin Way Teale believed that up until recently most people had some lonely spot where they could get away from it all, a little woodlot or streambank that engrained itself in the child's mind so that even in adulthood the place would endure in memory as an almost mystic domain, an enchanted spot somewhere at a remove from current existence.

I had a spot of that sort. Whose place it was, I never knew. The old estate building had burned, or was torn down or otherwise destroyed, and all that remained was the sad foundation and an apron of broken tiles that once served as a terrace, now overgrown with grass and struggling maple seedlings.

Beyond the terrace was a boxwood hedge gone wild and a shallow garden pool of broken moss-covered stone. The whole ruined garden was surrounded by a rich mid-Atlantic forest—great columns of sweet gum, beech, and tulip. And scattered within the gloom of the overarching trees were standing pergolas, broken pillars, the ruins of a garden house, and, most intriguing of all, an ancient swimming pool with a large puddle of standing water at the deep end, greenish with algae, occupied by golden-eyed frogs that dipped beneath the shadowy waters long before you could even think about catching them.

The ruins were perched on red cliffs high above the gray and dangerous river. I later learned the site was one of many such estates that had lined the cliffs in the bright years before the Crash. Here once dwelt the robber barons of Wall Street, and here now lay the evidence of their greed, a morass of cracked marble that served as a forbidden playground for wild bands of children.

The ruined garden still reappears in my dreams.

My friend Kata, who is a naturalist and basket maker, knows another such place. She grew up in Tiburon, across the bay from San Francisco, in the time when the now-fashionable community was a mere railroad town. Above her house, the high grassy hills of the north coast swept up to the sky, and here in her childhood she and her girl gang made grass huts in the hollows and gathered wildflowers: sticky monkey, lupine, poppies, and blue-eyed grass. One day there, alone on the peak of a hill under the vast sky, she saw an immense bird sweeping over the ridge and almost knocking her from her feet. It was not until Kata grew up that she realized it was probably a California condor. She still talks about the event.

Teale writes that he himself held a recollection of such a place.

He had been taken by his grandfather one snowy late autumn day to gather firewood. After a long horse-drawn sleigh ride through the empty landscape of fields and cut forest, the two of them came to an enchanted wood of oak, beech, hickory, ash, and sycamore. Here, while his grandfather loaded the cut wood, Teale, who was all of six years old at the time, wandered off down the vast hallways of the forest trees. An unidentifiable vaguely eerie atmosphere enveloped the dark forest; shrieks and mournful wailings sounded out in the empty landscape as the wind blew through the high branches. He was terrified, but enthralled, and carried on down the forested aisles, periodically returning to reassure himself that his grandfather was still there. He only visited the spot once, but the experience haunted him for years and in his adulthood he went back. He never could find it again.

The list of such experiences that have affected people who work in the field of natural history, or in fact anyone who still has an appreciation for wildness, must be as endless as it is varied—forested glens, solitary streambanks, small trash-littered pockets of urban lots, even, as in one case I know, the wild scrapings of an ailanthus branch on the window of a city apartment building on winter nights. The tragedy is that these semimystical childhood epiphanies are threatened in

our time and in danger of extinction. For a variety of reasons, children no longer wander alone or even in small bands out in the half-wild places that are often within walking distance of even the most urbanized environments. Part of the problem of course is technology, the lure of the computer, and video games, not to mention fear on the part of parents, instilled by the instant dissemination in the national news media of heinous crimes and perversions.

Some of the fears may be rational, although wilderness encounters always did have an element of danger. But one has to wonder, without the experience of such unstructured, unsupervised play, from what source will we draw the naturalists of the next generation.

Fall 2005

Night Life

Almost every day for more than twenty years now I have been going down to a bank above a slow stream where the bittern and the heron stalk the marshy reeds and otters slip through shadowy waters. I go in spring, when the stream is in full flood and the cries of red-winged blackbirds fill the air. I'm there in summer, when the forget-me-nots bloom and turtles bask along the banks. I come in autumn, when the marshes turn lion brown and flights of ducks crisscross the open sky. But, ironically, the best season to know the life along the stream is winter.

A few years ago on Christmas morning, long before anyone was up at home, I went down to my place beside the brook just before dawn. It was a day not unlike any of the 364 other days that I visit the place, except that this was the official beginning of winter and it had snowed the night before, leaving a light dusting that covered the ground and a clean blank slate whereon was written the stories of the night.

All the way down to the brook along an old cart road that leads from my house, I followed the tracks of a red fox that had apparently set out for its appointments of the night from the brushy field to the north. I noticed at one point that it stopped to investigate the signs (some of them invisible to me) left by other sojourners out on their various forays. At one point I noted that the fox halted to consider the footprints of another mammal before moving on—the round tracks of my own cat, who slept all day by the woodstove and then by night reverted to his primordial state and set out on night work of his own.

About halfway down to the brook, two coyotes came out of the swamps to the south, and nosed the tracks of the fox, and then moved on. (I noticed that they later circled around and ended up at the same place both the fox and I were headed—the stream bank.)

Three deer crossed the cartway about a hundred yards back from the banks, and everywhere in the surrounding woods I could see the little bastings of white-footed mouse tracks, stitching the trees together. At a gap in one of the old stone

walls that line the road a fisher had crossed and headed up the hill; next squirrels, more mice, the double print of a grouse wing (I think), a raccoon, and always along the whole route the fox, trotting at a determined pace and threading the whole tapestry of tracks together.

At various times during the night, most of these creatures—presumably the same ones I had seen in the upland—converged on the stream bank. Here there was a great mélange of comings and goings, snufflings in the snow, scratched stumps, droppings, the scent mound of a beaver, a scattering of seeds from foraging birds, the nipped twigs where rabbits and deer had fed, and a muddy slide where otters had slipped repeatedly into the dark waters. And all the while below the bank, I could see the as-yet-unfrozen black stream running down to its appointment with the sea.

Traditionally, the night that had just passed—the longest night of the year— was considered a dangerous time in the human community. Without the eternal intervention of priests and shamans, one could not be sure the sun would ever cease in its decline and rise again. But out in the wilder, perhaps more sensible, world, it was business as usual, a night like any other, filled with hunting and gathering and testing the territories for enemies, allies, or mates.

Winter 2005-2006

Of Floods and Folklore

Climate models based on the current rate of increase in greenhouse gases indicate that sea levels will rise at a rate of about two to five times the current rate over the next 100 years from the combined effect of ocean thermal expansion and increased glacier melt.

National Snow and Ice Data Center

Once upon a time, a small herd of woolly mammoths crossed over three sharp hills on the North American continent and moved eastward over a long plain covered with heather and crowberry. After some days they came to a high plateau where they remained long enough for one or two of them to have succumbed.

This was a scene that was repeated many times over the millennia. But in time the rains came and the waters rose and the high hills were covered and the waters prevailed upon the earth.

The high plateau at the edge of the continent is now known as Georges Bank. Fishing boats dragging the bank in the recent past have dredged up the bones of the mammoths that died there when it was dry land.

The three hills that once lay one hundred miles from the seacoast endured for thousands of years after the waters rose and even served as landmarks above a snug harbor first visited by a European named John Cabot in 1536. These same hills were subsequently leveled by English colonists and now survive, like so many natural landmarks, as a street name only—Tremont Street in this case—in the city now known as Boston.

The woolly mammoth itself is extinct and endures only in images scratched and painted on the cave walls of Perigord and in the folktales of the lost tribes of the North American Indians who once chased them across the dry plains east of Boston.

The waters that covered Georges Bank resulted from the melting of the ice walls of the late great glacier, some 11,000 years ago. We are now living at the end of a postglacial warming period, a time when, theoretically, the climate should

be cooling. But as we know (or at least as most of us know), the world climate is changing and the ice caps at the uttermost ends of the earth are melting and sea levels are rising again.

The record of the last great sea rise is fixed in the geological strata and can be read by scientists. But it is also true that the last great flooding occurred within the era of human consciousness. And, although the events associated with the flood took place in prehistorical times, before the advent of agriculture and the invention of the written word, the record of its coming and going is recorded in the folklore of the world. The story of a massive flood that covers the earth is an element of the folkloric histories of a wide variety of world cultures.

The Aboriginal Australians, members of one of the oldest extant cultures on earth, have any number of flood tales, ranging from the legend of a primordial snake that called for rain and caused the waters of the world to rise, to folktales in which rains fell for a long time until there was no dry land and all the people drowned. The Bahnar, who lived near Cochin in China, have a story in which a vengeful crab caused the sea and rivers to swell until the waters reached the sky. The only survivors were a brother and sister who took one pair each of all the earth's animals with them in a huge chest.

Here in the West, the first written epic, the Sumerian tale of Gilgamesh, set down some 6,000 years ago, has at its core the story of a great flood. The Hebrews told the same story in the narrative of Noah and the Ark, and the Hindu culture recorded the account of a fish who warned Manu, the first human, of the coming of a great deluge and told him to build a ship to save himself and the animals.

And so it goes, down through the ages: rising waters, and a few, ethical, wise human beings who save the world for the future.

The point is there is nothing unnatural or unusual about floods. The problem seems to be that, for all our histories and our record keeping and folklore, people seem to have short memories and tend to settle in floodplains as soon as the waters recede.

Now in our time, with the waters rising again, we continue the practice, trusting in nothing more than suspect technologies to save us from the flood next time.

Spring 2006

Archeology of the Garden

Last spring, in the process of digging out a new garden bed, I turned up the rib bone of a horse. It was about two feet long, yellowed with age, pocked and scribed, and much gnawed by mice, and it had been weathered by soils and long winters. Hefting it absentmindedly there in the spring sunshine—it suddenly struck me—I think I knew this horse.

When I first moved to this property nearly thirty years ago, the land in this section was a dark forest of white pine, a veritable desert, it seemed to me, where nothing other than a few starflowers and sarsaparilla grew and no birds sang. One day shortly after I moved onto the land, a large red-haired man of about 60 showed up at the front door and asked if he could have a look around. He said that he had grown up in the house as part of a large extended family. One night in the mid-1930s, when he was about 16, he and a cousin lowered themselves out of an upstairs bedroom window and hit the road. This was his first time back in forty odd years.

We took a walk around the land while he reminisced about his childhood years on this small subsistence farm. The greatest shock to him was the white pine stand. In his time that section of the property had been an apple orchard. Among his many stories was one involving a half-wild white horse that no one could saddle. He and his friends used to jump on its back and go dashing bareback through the orchard while the horse would try to dislodge them by running under low-lying branches. Later, the horse went blind and spent its last years grazing under the apple trees, and when it finally died his family hauled it up to the back wall and buried it.

Over the thirty-year period that I have lived on this land, little by little, stone by stone, I have slowly cleared the stand of white pines to make room for new gardens, a decidedly unenvironmentally sound practice save for the fact that there now seem to be more birds and more wildlife in the gardens than there were in the dark pines. In the process of all that digging and delving, I have turned up much evidence of the various families that have lived on this land since 1810 when the house was built: shoe leather, old tools, medicine bottles, ink bottles, buttons, shards of willowware, shards of Canton china, bits of glass, bits of stoneware, pottery, clay marbles, a doll's foot, knives and forks, and leaky tin pots. Also arrowheads. This was apple country, the Nashoba Valley, one of the oldest extant farming regions in New England, having been worked by the English since 1654, and for nearly 3,000 years before that by the Indians. In fact, Christianized Indians planted the first apple trees in the valley: Roxbury Russets brought over by John Winthrop in 1630.

The first arrowhead I found was a nondescript modest point from what was known as the Late Woodland culture, a very recent group as far as Native American history is concerned. But just over the hill there are two working farms (the last of the five that remained when I first came here). The new farmers— which is to say, the English, Germans, Italians, and Greeks who worked this land over the 352-year period—would turn up arrowheads during spring plowing. Some of these were saved at the local historical society, and, with a little care, you can work backward through the buried layers of Native American history, ending with a singular point that now resides in the collection, a so-called Paleo point, about five inches long with a fluted groove down the center.

In the time of the Paleo people, the garden patch where I found the horse bone was a dry grassy hill at the eastern end of a shallow lake. Moving across the landscape were mastodons, giant elk, barren ground caribou, and other species of Pleistocene megafauna, all of which the Indians hunted. Slowly, over the millennia, as the climate changed, the human uses of the land changed. Hunting and plant gathering declined, and about 3,000 years ago was slowly overtaken and eventually replaced by agriculture. Now agriculture is in decline. Most of the old orchards are gone, save for one publicly owned patch that was acquired by the town. The farmers who still work these agricultural lands might as well work for nonprofit agencies, such is their income, and slowly, farm by farm, field by field, and lot by lot, new houses and small electronic-based industries have moved in. Nothing new in all this—it's an old story. Changes in the land.

But in our time the old story is also a new story since there are now also

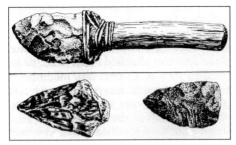

changes in the climate, which is what drove the original cultural evolution of this part of the world. And yet, in an ironic and atavistic twist, old patterns endure: there are still horses here. In fact, there are a lot of horses.

This too fits a land use pattern.

One of the phenomena of the so-called edge cities—the burgeoning computer-based development patterns at highway intersections just beyond the old core cities—is that just outside the edge cities, in the nation of the great mega-mansions, there are also horse pastures for the weekend entertainment of executives of those industries.

Furthermore, in spite of the changing economic conditions, there are still—somehow—real farms. In fact, according the USDA, one of the fast-growing segments of American farm economies is the peri-urban agriculture, that is, small specialized farms within thirty miles of big cities.

And finally, in those few small patches of private and public woodlands and fields, where they are permitted to follow their primordial tradition, there are, ironically, still a few hunters. One of the heralds of autumn in this section of the town is the early-morning sound of duck hunters' gunfire from down in the marshes of Beaver Brook, which runs east of my house.

And all the while, things accumulate in the soils beneath: car parts, farm equipment, bottles, china plates, horse bones, arrowheads. Walk the woods in these parts and you walk over history. And walls, of course—walls everywhere. But also foundations, forgotten roads, beds of daffodils, patches of vinca, and, in one corner I know, a fine stand of flowering peonies. Custom lies beneath your feet. But custom appears to accumulate in the human psyche as well as in the form of hunters and farmers, and gardeners who feel the need to clear land to grow vegetables and flowers.

Ultimately, perhaps a long memory saves land.

Autumn 2006

Forever Common

In 1652, John Eliot, the so-called prophet of the Indians, having successfully converted a mixed band of Native Americans to the Christian faith, granted the group a sixteen-square-mile tract of land just northwest of Concord to be called Nashobah Plantation. The Indians set up a village of English-style frame houses; planted their fields in corn, beans, and squash; and, having cut their hair and agreed to wear shoes, settled in to live in the English manner.

Like many of their people, the tribe had no clear concept of ownership of land. Over the millennia in North America, they had evolved a system of land use that was based on rights of use rather than outright ownership. At a yearly council, the leader of the tribe would assign certain portions of a territory to certain family groups for a specific use, such as berry picking or hunting. Sometimes the rights of use would even overlap, so that one family could hunt deer in a given area but not pick the blueberries whereas another family, using the same section, could pick the blueberries but not hunt the deer. It was a good system; the lands were allotted according to the availability of game or fruits and were assigned to ensure sustainability.

But unfortunately, the practice, which had evolved over a period of some 3,000 years, was about to come to an end.

With the outbreak of King Philip's War in 1675, in spite of the Nashobah Indians' Christianity and their allegiance to the English, colonists relocated them to Deer Island in Boston Harbor where many succumbed to starvation. After the war, the people dispersed; only one or two returned to Nashobah; and in 1725, the last known survivor, a woman named Sarah Doublet, sold the remaining 500 acres of land at the core of the plantation to a family from Concord named Jones.

Under the English governance, the tract did not exactly belong to the Jones family. The property was theoretically "owned" by the King of England. Not unlike the Indians, the Jones had leased the rights of use. But after the American Revolution, the pattern of land control changed yet again, and the 500 acres of the original sixteen-square-mile plantation were divided and sold and owned outright by the various parties in fee simple, as the phrase has it. No strings attached. In theory, the owners could do what they liked with the property—which, until zoning regulations came along in the 1950s—they did.

Fortunately, over 320 years of private ownership the various proprietors proved to be good stewards. They maintained farms and orchards, specializing in apples, Berkshire hogs, and Holstein cows. By the late 1800s, the whole Nashobah Valley, of which this plot was a part, was devoted mostly to apples. In 1905, more apples were exported from this region than from anywhere else in New England—mostly to Britain.

Then in the late 1950s, just when the farms and the orchards in the Nashobah Valley were beginning to decline, a single owner got ahold of the entire 500-acre plot where the Christian Indian village had been located and began to restore the declining orchards. He grew peaches and introduced new varieties of apples and made use of innovative growing techniques, including methods designed to reduce pesticide use; and when he died, in 1986, it was learned that he had written a covenant into his will—the land could only be legally sold for agricultural use.

By the 1990s, there was a new crop sprouting in the Nashoba Valley, this one obliquely related to another sort of apple—i.e., the computer. No buyers were interested in land for farming. But the town had been given the right of first refusal on the property, and after very little debate at town meeting the orchard was saved.

As a result of that purchase, this isolated, otherwise unremarkable, little tract offers an instructive lesson on the nature of land use. For as many as 3,000 years under Indian management, the tract was basically common land, open to use to anyone in the tribe—with restrictions. During the 150-year control of the English, it was granted by the Crown—with restrictions. Then it was privately held for 300 years. Now it is common land again—also with restrictions.

But whether private or Crown or common, as a result of sound stewardship by three different cultures, the basic ecological structure of the land, the woods, fields, orchards, and lakeshore has endured.

Winter 2007-2008

Lost in the Stars

On warm summer nights when the smell of the river marshes below the house would fill the air and dusk had long since faded out, we would sit on the front porch, watching the fireflies flashing in the hayfields to the west. My family—uncles, aunties, distant cousins, friends of cousins, cousins of friends of cousins—would sit and rock and talk about crops and dogs, horses, and hot weather. The air was thick then, and summer had its grip on us, and sometimes, it seemed to me, the very house would lift from its foundation at these hours and float suspended above the drying grasses and the fields to the north where the corn rustled in the evening wind.

On nights such as this, as the fireflies ascended, my old father would often reminisce about his years in the Orient, and as winking stars of light rose in the fields below us he would retell yet again the old Japanese folktale of Princess Firefly and recount stories of the traditional firefly festivals that took place all over Japan in his time.

I was lost in the mystery of all this and would be swept into some vague, almost timeless suspension of disbelief. It all seemed so real, even though my father was telling the story of a firefly that was in fact a princess in a kingdom inhabited by insects. I was too young to know it was not true.

And often on those hot nights, as children have done for thousands of years, my cousins and I would descend from the porch with kitchen jars and sweep the grasses, catching the flashers and carrying them around in the jars like mystic lanterns.

Timing seemed everything to me, even then. Why did the fireflies flash at certain intervals? Why did they quit flashing periodically, and why did some of them never take to the air and perch low in the grasses, emitting a long, sustained light?

It was only later that I learned that there was a dark side to the luminous display taking place in the fields below the house, and that all the bright poetic legends and folktales had an element of truth. Out there in the real world of the grassroot

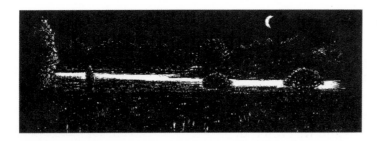

jungle, the lights that so inspired the folktales and festivals were in fact all about sex and death.

Fireflies flash to attract mates, and it is for the most part the males that we see on summer nights. Shortly after they reach adulthood, usually around late June in New England, as dusk falls, the males launch themselves in the air and patrol to-and-fro across open areas, flashing a semaphoric signal to female fireflies, who lie below, watching. There are as many as thirty different species of firefly in New England, and the males of each species have a set pattern of flashes, which the female can recognize.

Below in the grasses, females spotting a potential mate light up with a sustained flash. The male blazes back, the female lights up again, and, after a series of exchanges, the male descends to locate his mate. Sometimes more than one suitor will fly down and the firefly princess will be surrounded by a company of suitors, each flashing handsome signals. But fireflies, it appears, are discreet denizens of this untamed complex world. Once the couple has found each other the lights go out and they mate.

All is not love in the world of fireflies, however; there is also the question of sustenance. There is one species of firefly that makes use of the flashing repertoire of males to attain a meal. These carnivorous femmes fatales lie low in the grass and watch for the signals of other species of males flashing above. They imitate the flash pattern, and thereby draw the unsuspecting male down to his demise.

But all that is science. When you are ten years old, and it is night, and the sparking stars of fireflies drift over the hay fields, and the wind is in the corn, it is all a half-lit poetic mystery.

Summer 2008

A Moveable Feast

$\mathcal{S}$ome years ago I set out to see if I could walk from Westford to Concord without ever resorting to paved roads—of which there were many along my intended route.

The plan required a certain amount of what Henry Thoreau used to call cross-lot walking, which in our time we would define more prosaically as trespassing. It also required, at least in my case, a good sense of direction. Lacking such contemporary navigational devices such as a Garmin GPSMAP or smartphone, and armed solely with a knowledge of the lay of the land, the position of the sun, and a sadly out-of-date geodetic survey map, I was delightfully lost from time to time, which was part of the idea. I wanted to imagine, as did Mr. Thoreau, the possibility of encountering some remnant of wildness in my own backyard.

This venture took place on Columbus Day, a holiday set aside to celebrate the arrival of the first of many alien invasive animals and plants in this brave new world of the Americas; and as I forged through swamps and thickets, deep forests of hemlock and pine, and uplands of hardwoods, I did in fact encounter many exotic plant species, as well as a number of people of European ancestry and a bird or two of British origin. But I also came across many native plants, and inasmuch as this was autumn and all the leaves were ablaze and the day was bright and the weather warm, it seemed to me at times that I was passing through a veritable Eden of abundance.

Ripeness was all that day. Even before I set out, I noticed a patch of bright red *Russula* mushrooms, and a little farther along a cluster of oyster mushrooms, a puffball, and a fine stand of coral fungi. Then, not a quarter of a mile onward, having crossed the first of some five or six roads I would traverse that day, I came upon someone's neglected summer garden, all overgrown with the drupes and seeds and berries of various European and Asian species of plants. Thirty yards beyond the garden I came to an immigration story of a different sort—an apple orchard.

Although there was a native crabapple here in North America before the seventeenth century, the Reverend William Blackstone, the first European settler in the place that became Boston, brought a bag of apple seeds with him and planted an orchard on Beacon Hill. The governor of the Boston Puritan colony, John Winthrop, who arrived five years after Blackstone, in 1630, was himself an orchardist back in Suffolk. He took over Blackstone's orchard and brought over his own supply of pips, or apple seeds, as well as honeybees for pollination. These he developed into the Roxbury Russet, the first of the New World apples; and since these modest beginnings American growers have developed several hundred varieties of apple.

On the eastern edge of the orchard, effectively blocking my intended passage, was a thicket of blackberry canes so dense and so impenetrable that I was forced to cast about for a suitable route to the east. In the end, the only way through was a wide clearing covered with another berry-producing plant—poison ivy. But I slogged on.

All along the way as I wove through the landscape I came upon similar thickets of berries and wide patches of poison ivy, as well as old struggling apple trees growing in deep shaded woods of white pine, or maple and hickory. I also crossed over many stone walls and hedgerows festooned with vines and ramblers. Here was the native fox grape, the original species from which Ephraim Wales Bull developed the famous Concord grape in the midnineteenth century. Here also was the rambling riverbank grape, known more simply as the frost grape. In the green tangles of Virginia creeper and in the wooded sections, I tramped through stands of shagbark hickory, pignut, beech, and butternut, and sections of woods strewn with the acorns of black oak and red oak. The nuts of all these trees once served as crucial fare for the native people of this country as well as the European colonists.

Like most hunter-gatherer cultures, the Native Americans were skilled at plant identification and use. Somewhere within the town of Acton (I think), I came to a dry hillside covered with blueberry bushes, one of the staples of their diet. The tribes in this region used to practice an early form of game management that involved the shrub. The Indians would burn over certain sections of the forest to encourage berry growth, which would in turn encourage the local populations of the white-tailed deer and black bear, both of which they would hunt. In preparation for winter, the local Indians would make a trail food known as pemmican by mixing blueberries with bear fat and strips of dried venison.

I once knew a man who claimed that with three milk goats and a working knowledge of edible wild plants an individual could live comfortably off the land throughout the year. He happened to live in Arizona, and I doubt that he and his goats could survive a New England winter, but I did come across many wild edible plants on my walk that day: elderberries; five different species of edible mushrooms that I was able to identify, and many more that I couldn't; acorns, which the Indians would boil and dry and grind for flour; and also ubiquitous stands of lamb's-quarters, a plant that the Indians would eat as a green in spring and as a ground seed meal in winter. The seeds of this plant are notoriously abundant—as many as 75,000 on a single plant—and are common in local archeological digs. I also passed isolated stands of American filbert, or hazelnut, a favorite of both mice and men. In some obscure history, I remember reading that the whole army of some ten thousand knights and soldiers of King Henry V, marching toward Agincourt, was sustained for a day or two with the local species of hazelnut.

Somewhere near Butter Brook in Acton—or maybe Concord (nature knows nothing of political boundaries)—I came upon another lesser known staple of both the Indians and the newly arrived Puritans: the groundnut. It may be that there were more groundnuts in the primal forests of New England—old histories describe an abundance of vines of these underground tuberous plants bearing "nuts" as large as small potatoes, and records indicate that along with the tubers of hog peanut, which I also saw all along my route, groundnuts were an important fall crop.

It was not only human fare that I passed during that singular journey. Most of the plants that I encountered served also to feed the local wildlife as well.

Autumn, when the fruits and berries and nuts are ripe, is the most abundant season. Some common plants, such as poison ivy, which provides sustenance for some fifty species of birds and mammals, are unappreciated, even despised, by the human community. And some, such as blackberry and blueberry, are valued by both wildlife and people. Blackberries and their kin—along with raspberries, serviceberries, and chokeberries—feed any number of local songbirds including waxwings, bluebirds, grosbeaks, and tanagers, not to mention bears, one of which earlier that year had passed through these highly suburbanized lands. Blueberries, also a favorite of bears, sustain to some extent or another about fifty species, including chipmunks and mice, as well as upland game birds.

By dusk, much scratched, tired, and with soaked feet, I finally reached the long sanctuary of Concord's Estabrook Woods, a favorite food-gathering haunt of Henry Thoreau.

It was here that Thoreau encountered one of the great characters of his writings: old Brooks Clark, who was headed home that day with his collected wild fare. He was barefooted, carrying his shoes stuffed with "knurly" wild apples and a dead robin. Trails in the Estabrook were clear and easy to follow, but emerging out of the woods I found the only way to town center was to tred through the historic well-traveled byways and public paths of Concord.

To cap things off, at the end of the walk when my shuttle driver arrived to take me home, we settled in for an evening meal at the Colonial Inn, which happened to be celebrating autumn on its menu with servings of local fare—butternut squash, roast pork with applesauce, duckling with a blueberry sauce, mulled cider, and Indian pudding.

We accompanied this hearty repast that evening with a French Burgundy, a wine made, incidentally, from grape varieties that were saved from extinction in the midnineteenth century by the rootstocks of the native American fox grape.

Such is the so-called Columbian Exchange. We get alien plants and apples; Europe gets the potato, the tomato, and restored vineyards.

Autumn 2008

The Names of Wind

According to the Western Abenaki of New England, the winds of their world were generated by a giant eagle that lived on a craggy peak and flapped its wings continuously. Various nomadic tribes of central Asia had a comparable myth. They believed that the wind originated from a vast hole in a mountain somewhere to the west. And the Inuit of Alaska thought that the winds issued forth from an opening in the sky.

Here in the West, we believe that the wind is generated by the mother of all earthly things, our own star Sun. According to our legend, the sun beats down on the equatorial tropics, heating the air, which subsequently rises high into the stratosphere, creating a vacuum all along the equator. Because of the physical phenomenon known as the Coriolis effect, air from both the north and the south rushes in to fill the space, thereby creating, because of the rotation of the earth, the ever-reliable trade winds.

This basic system is much complicated by landforms such as deserts and mountain ranges, which churn and blend the moving airs, creating a variety of local winds. Some of these such as the foehn are warm dry winds that flow down the lee side of the mountains. Some, such as the sirocco, are bred in deserts and drawn northward by low-pressure areas. Many of these local winds are notorious for their strength as well as their effect on the human psyche, and most of them are named, a fact that has added to the rich tapestry of languages.

For a while, when I was younger, I lived in one of the epicenters of these local wind systems—the island of Corsica, which is tucked up in the northeastern corner of the Mediterranean and for this reason is subject to powerful winds from both the European continent and North Africa. It is probably not coincidental that the first place Odysseus fetched up after his sailors mistakenly released the four winds that set him on his twenty-year course of wanderings was likely Corsica.

Nine winds plague the island. In winter the chilling mistral comes scything down the Rhône Valley, lifting tiles from roofs and screaming across the Gulf of Genoa to Corsica, where it is sometimes joined, or followed, by a companion wind called the tramontana, which blasts in off the cold plains of the Po. The

sirocco charges up from the Sahara, carrying desert sands and hammering at the island as many as a hundred days a year. The grecale brings rain from the Apennines every winter. The levante storms in from the east. The ponente from the west. The mezzogiorno at midday and the terrana blows in at dusk, reaching its crescendo at midnight. And finally, there is the libecciu, the sickle of the northwest coast, where I lived. It crosses the Mediterranean and comes cutting in from Gibraltar, slamming itself against Cap Corse and beating the sea to a froth.

The winds of Corsica are an annoyance, but, except perhaps for the cold, bright, headache-inducing mistral, they do not seem to affect the islanders' frame of mind. Farther to the east, that is not the case. The meltemi, which is associated with bad tempers, screams out of the Balkans and strikes at the Isles of Greece. The traditional hot suffocating simoon breeds in the deserts of the Arabian Peninsula, carrying the dust and sand of the Sahara and causing shortness of breath and fretfulness; and to the west, in Niger, the dusty harmattan is believed to agitate local cattle. People in Austria and southern Germany say they can feel the onset of the mountain wind known as the foehn, which brings on a general lethargy, headaches, irritability, and may even be associated with thrombosis. And there is a northerly wind in Spain, the matacabras, that supposedly kills goats.

Here in North America, we do not lack our own ill winds. In southern California, the fire-breeding Santa Ana brings on asthma and hay fever and carries thick clouds of smoke and ash from its associated fires. In Texas, the clear sky-blue northers often signify an ominous change in the weather, and the famous warming wind of the eastern Rockies, known as the Chinook, or snow eater, can melt a foot of snow in a matter of hours, bring on migraines, and may even have an effect on crime rates.

Fortunately, here in fickle-weathered New England, we only have two winds to fear—the rainy southeasters and the dreaded northeasters—which give rise to high winds and heavy rains, or snow or sleet or freezing rain, and sink ships, erode beaches, and bring on an internal chill that even tea and a warm fireplace cannot seem to banish.

Summer 2009

Bygone Birds

I grew up in a town famous for its old trees and gardens and also for its birdlife. There was a landscaped hillside visible from my bedroom, and one of my earliest memories is of the vast rolling chorus of robins, doves, and thrushes, and the unidentifiable (at least to me) squeaks, squawks, chips, buzzings, and peeps that would pour in my window like a waterfall on spring mornings.

I never thought about this great choral expression; it was just there, part of my world.

My family had come north from the Eastern Shore of Maryland, and, on summer visits to the rural settings of the old family farms and town gardens, the dawn chorus of birds was equally loud—as was the daylong winsome calling of the bobwhites and the noisy barking of crows in flocks that would dip across the cornfields. At night on my cousin's river farm, I lay awake listening to the dark quock of night-herons sounding out from the riverbanks, and by day we lived with the eternal circling cries of ospreys. I even used to see bald eagles there, a rare event back then.

After that I lived in deep woods in northwestern Connecticut, where there were vast migrations of wood-warblers each spring and fall. That was owl country; the odd caterwauls of barred owls rang out from the nearby swampy lowlands in autumn and again in spring. I would hear the ghostly whinny of the screech-owl all through the summer, and the deep booming of the great horned owl on late winter nights, along with other shrieks and calls. Also on summer nights there, I used to be awakened by the mysterious night song of the ovenbird, along with the shrills and snarls and cries of things I couldn't identify—probably bobcats.

When I first moved to Massachusetts thirty or so years ago, I lived in an old house surrounded by farms. Each spring, the scrubby pasture just north of the house was loud with the calls of prairie warblers and blue-winged warblers. All along the brushy edges of the property, yellow warblers and yellowthroats nested. The indigo buntings would be singing madly by June, and every day the woodland edges were pierced with the sharp call of the great crested flycatcher. I used to see kingbirds in a nearby orchard; while the woods to the west, just beyond the garden wall, were alive with the songs of veeries, wood thrushes, ovenbirds, and black-and-white warblers, as well as ruby-crowned kinglets and parula warblers. And east of the house, hay fields dropped down to the marshes of Beaver Brook in a series of terraces, over which barn swallows and tree swallows coursed from dawn to dusk. Wood ducks, hooded mergansers, marsh wrens, green herons, and even the occasional bittern and sora rail used to appear in the marshes from time to time.

At dawn last spring, I heard the song of a black-billed cuckoo. That got me thinking about local birds. How long ago had it been since I last heard a black-billed cuckoo in the yard? For that matter, how long had it been since I had heard the plaintive dawn song of the wood pewee? Or the night wailing of the whip-poor-will? This year, other than the music of a black-billed cuckoo, and one ovenbird, plus the usual array of garden birds such as blue jays and song sparrows, it was a silent spring. Furthermore, I have revisited most of the places I lived in the past and have noted the same phenomenon. The woods and fields have gone to development, and no birds sing.

All this is anecdotal evidence, but it's a story you hear over and over. And now the facts of a massive worldwide decline of birds are everywhere in the scientific news. It appears that the whole class of aves, a group that emerged some 150 million years ago, for a variety of reasons, is at a low ebb.

Fall 2009

The Earth as Vernal Pool

On a warming afternoon around the beginning of March last spring, I heard the first calls from a population of wood frogs that collect in a series of vernal pools on the northwest side of my property. Their ducklike quacking, along with the appearance of mourning cloak butterflies, and the spearing heads of skunk cabbage in the local swamps, is a reliable indication of the advent of true spring. But the last few years have been uncertain. Dry spells have become more common, even in spring, and for whatever reason the pools have been drying out earlier than usual, threatening the year's crop of frogs. Last spring was the worst of these years.

The season started well enough: the snows melted, the ice went out of the pools, and the wood frogs arrived on schedule and began calling. By April 1, I could see the submerged twigs and branches. But around mid-April, the rains ceased and we entered into a dry spell, coupled with some strange unseasonably high temperatures. The pond edges began to shrink. The heat and drought continued into May, and soon enough it looked like the pools would dry out, even before the eggs hatched.

I'm not sure of the legality, or even the wisdom, of what followed, but I set out on a campaign to rescue at least a segment of the population. I have three different ornamental pools in my garden, two of them heavily vegetated and deep enough to maintain cool waters. So little by little I began collecting eggs from the vernal pools and moving them to my own pools. I had help in this from a willing five year old, and three or four times a week we would carry a net and buckets to the vernal pools, scoop up a mass of eggs, and carry them back to the garden.

Our rescue operation continued all through May. And all the while, the heat and the drought wore on, and the pools diminished day by day, foot by foot, leaving a surround of wet vegetation.

Nonetheless, at some point during that month some of the eggs hatched; I could see the little tadpoles in the deeper water. The boy and I would wait and watch for wiggling ripples in the still waters and then scoop them out with the nets and carry the tadpoles back to the garden pools.

As the vernal pools dried, this rescue operation began to take on a bit of a desperate maneuver. By early June, with still no significant rain, the center of the pools was no more than a mud puddle teeming with wriggling tadpoles. And beyond these last refuges, in the drying leaves, we could find multitudes of those unfortunates that did not survive. We began going out every morning, bringing in more and more survivors. Finally, as far as we could tell, there were no more struggling tadpoles in the now-dried-out pools.

Meanwhile the ones we had rescued thrived. Slowly over the month of June and early July the tadpoles grew legs. We checked their progress by netting them to watch the growth of their legs and the slow shrinking of their tails. Happily, as the season progressed, there seemed to be fewer and fewer in the pools—presumably a good sign. They were making their way out into the wide world.

Then, late in the summer, along with the usual adults that seem to appear at the end of the growing season each year, I began spotting tiny wood frogs, more than usual.

I see a metaphor in all this. Without our intervention that season's crop of local frogs would not have thrived, thereby decreasing, however slightly, the number of wood frogs in the world. The adults that originally laid the eggs will probably return to their native ponds this year, and the year after. But in an increasingly warming planet, and with the associated vagaries of bizarre weather, who knows how long that population would last? So our efforts, for the time being, were justified.

But in a sense, the earth is a vernal pool. The climate is warming, habitats are disappearing worldwide, populations of wild things are shrinking, and there are no godlike giants roaming the earth to scoop us up and carry us off to a better more sustainable planet.

Spring 2014